Planning Your Internet Marketing Strategy

Planning Your Internet Marketing Strategy

A DOCTOR EBIZ® GUIDE

Ralph F. Wilson

John Wiley & Sons, Inc.

Published by John Wiley & Sons, Inc., New York.

Published simultaneously in Canada.

Library of Congress Cataloging-in-Publication Data:

Wilson, Ralph F., 1945–
   Planning your internet marketing strategy : a Doctor Ebiz guide / Ralph F. Wilson
     p. cm.
   Includes bibliographical references and index.
   ISBN 0-471-44109-0 (paper: alk. paper)
   1. Internet marketing—Planning. 2. Electronic commerce—Planning. 3. Strategic planning. I. Title.
HF5415.1265.W55 2001
658.8'4—dc21

2001D26304

Printed in the United States of America

10 9 8 7 6 5 4 3 2 1

To Jean, the girl next door, my high school sweetheart, and my lifelong companion.

Contents

Part II.   Situation Analysis

Part III. Market and Product Focus

Part V.   Putting It All Together

Acknowledgments

Trying to keep up with the speeding development curve of Internet business in the past six years has required continuous learning from my many friends and colleagues.

I'll name just a few, but there are many, many unnamed: Larry Chase, Dan Janal, John Audette, Dana Blankenhorn, Ken Evoy, Jim Sterne, the columnists at ClickZ, and many whose article URLs fill my online research database and whose volumes fill my bookshelves. Kevin Elliott, one of my link editors, has pointed me to many resources I otherwise wouldn't have known about. I've learned a lot from my clients, too, especially Joanne Gucwa, one of my earliest clients and now a collaborator on several projects.

My three children, David, Dan, and Ann, have worked with me in my business over the years and have added real quality to the enterprise. My wife, Jean, has been a wise counselor, and has shown great patience with my long hours.

One of the joys of the Internet is having a huge network of friends covering the globe. I really feel the goodwill of thousands of newsletter readers plugging for me, encouraging me on, and recommending my work to others. They are constantly sharing with me insights and new angles on e-business.

Most of all I am thankful to God, who saw fit to put me in the right place at the right time and who is my constant friend.

Introduction

Millions of dollars are squandered every year because businesspeople like you and me refuse to look honestly and clearly at our businesses. We go from day to day doing what we must—ordering, paying bills, selling, putting out fires. But because we put off planning, our businesses struggle and dwindle.

In this book we'll be talking about the marketing planning process. A formal business plan includes more detail in certain areas. But of necessity we need to examine whether or not your business will be viable on the Web from a marketing standpoint. As we study the various aspects, if you'll put aside time to do the planning steps I'm outlining, you'll find your online business energized—or perhaps radically changed—in a period of a few months. Each chapter concludes with a hands-on exercise.

We need to start at the beginning, at the strategic planning level. Now if you're in a large corporation, you may not have much control over decisions at this level. But if you have responsibility for the e-business aspect of your company, if you're a small businessperson with an existing business, or if you're planning an Internet start-up, this is where you must begin.

If you need to write a formal Internet Marketing Plan, we'll show you just how to do that. But even if you don't have to write a formal Internet Marketing Plan for your boss or to obtain funding, the discipline of writing your own Plan will pay you rich rewards in success, and help you avoid serious mistakes that you'd never uncover without this rigorous approach. So I suggest writing down what you're learning; the process of writing will make you more curious and more careful.

This book isn't about promoting a web site. Promotion comes at the tail-end of marketing planning. But the work you do in planning will determine whether promotion will do any good at all.

This book is about nitty-gritty marketing planning as it applies to an online business. If you think that optimizing web pages to please search engines is what Web marketing is all about, then you're about to have your eyes opened. Reach for your dark glasses to cut the glare, and get ready to read!

I wish you every success—business, personal, and spiritual.

Part I
Strategic Planning

It's easy to underestimate or overestimate the Internet. Now, after a number of years of commercial use, we have some idea of what it can and can't do—at least with current approaches. But we are captives of our own experience and ways of thinking. In this section I want to give you some new lenses through which to view the Internet and your own business, to systematically work out the purposes your web site should fulfill in your business, and to see the opportunity for niches where new and improved Internet businesses can prosper.

Chapter 1

Comprehending the Opportunities for Doing Business on the Web

Prepare to expand your thinking. Before we begin to plan, let's look at some of the possibilities available. Here are six different ways to look at the Internet business opportunity.

Once there was life without drive-up fast food. Hard to imagine, I know, but true. I called my local Burger King manager and asked, "How much of your business goes out the drive-up window?"

"More than 50%," he told me.

I expect, though, that to restaurants used to a sit-down business, opening a drive-up window seemed pretty radical. It involved a whole new way of understanding the food store business. But now it's taken for granted among fast food giants.

Doing business on the Web requires the same kind of quantum leap. It's hard to get your head around it right away, since it is so different from what you've been used to. My 94-year-old mother won a state championship for typing speed when she was in high school. But we have this conversation occasionally:

"Ralph, just what is it you do?"
"I do business on the Internet, Mom."
"What's the Internet? Is that like broadcasting to people?"
"Well, sort of. . . ."

I get no further, since she has no real point of comparison.

No, I'm not going to introduce the Internet to you. But I hope to offer points of comparison that convey six opportunities the Internet opens to your business.

■ Opportunity 1.   Branch Office

Newbies see the Internet as advertising. But a business web site is better understood as a branch office, a place of doing business. It's like opening a second office where you can entertain customers, except this office has the lights on and coffee ready 24 hours a day, seven days per week. People can stop in at their convenience any time they want and browse through your offerings. They'll:

- Read the brochures in the rack by the door.
- Pick up a copy of your "Common Questions People Ask about Our Business."
- Solve their own problems with your detailed Troubleshooting Guide.
- Scribble messages on the pad of question forms you've provided.
- Look at detailed information and specs about each product you offer, and
- Make vending machine purchases in your lobby, day or night.

What's the rent? Somewhere between $20 to $100 per month for smaller businesses. And the initial build-out of your branch office costs only a few thousand dollars. Sure, you'll need to remodel every year or two to keep it up-to-date. But that's a small price to pay for the new customers your branch office will bring.

Remember, don't think "advertising," think "branch office," and you'll begin to grasp the Internet opportunity.

■ Opportunity 2.   World Market

I'm amazed by how many people are blind to the second business opportunity the Internet offers—a world market. Not too long ago a medium-size mail-order executive told me, "The boss insists that we need to prevent people from other countries from ordering on our new site. We just don't do much international business, and it's a pain to ship outside the country." I gritted my teeth and tried to smile.

A rapidly increasing number of people around the world use the Internet to purchase items they can't find locally. In early 2001, for example, 22.5 million Chinese are now connected to the Internet, along with 2.6 million from India and 2.1 million Malaysians. Twelve million in France are now online, and nearly half the population of Sweden. Israel boasts 1.25 million Internet users, and the list goes on and on.

If you're fast on your feet, you have the opportunity to make some of them your customers. Don't know how to market to those abroad? You'll find lots of free information online (such as www.wilsonweb.com/cat/cat.cfm?page = 1&subcat = mm _Global). Don't neglect the resources your national government provides. They want to help you bring more money flowing into your country.

Think about it. The Internet provides a small business in Peoria, Illinois, or Istanbul, Turkey, the opportunity to be a global company with little expenditure except time given to learning. On the Internet, geography has ceased to be a barrier. A small business market used to be limited to a one-hour drive from its store or office. No more. People now shop a global directory on the Web and let the best site win.

Of course, some products don't lend themselves to a global market. Take pizza, for example. Can you imagine delivery of a flat box containing two-day-old pepperoni with anchovies? Gross! When I first began to write and speak about the Internet in 1995, I'd say, "If you sell pizza, you probably won't do well on the Internet." Then I heard about Pizza Hut in Santa Cruz, California, taking orders from students at the nearby University of California campus. The store hurdled convenience barriers (busy signals on a Friday night) and propelled this savvy local business to increased sales.

Brainstorm, my friends. Dream! A global opportunity awaits you.

■ Opportunity 3.   Direct Sales

A third opportunity is direct sales, jumping the existing distribution chain that ratchets up prices to the end user.

Many online-only businesses are essentially order-taking front offices. Product fulfillment is through manufacturers and distributors who agree to drop-ship directly to the customer. This way Web retailers don't incur expenses for inventory and warehousing. (Nor do they have the ability for superior customer service, but that's another story.)

A really scary development to many manufacturers is the

growing temptation for them to sell directly on the Web and bypass the complex distribution chain they have built over many years. The manufacturer doesn't want to anger distributors and dealers. But, increasingly, competing manufacturers sell direct from the factory and undercut the price to the end user. For many manufacturers, it's a decision to either sell directly or lose market share. Agony! What do you do when the Dell Computer equivalent in your industry sells directly over the Web, pulls in many millions of dollars per day in revenue, and grows faster than any other competitor? You sweat bullets, and finally bite the bullet. (Oh, the agony of mixed metaphors!)

Direct retail sales via the Internet is growing exponentially. What an opportunity for your business!

■ Opportunity 4. Networking

Why does a company network its desktop computers? To increase communication, collaboration, and productivity. The Internet networks half the computers in the world.

Think of the possibilities. Now Bern, Switzerland, is closer to Abu Dhabi, United Arab Emirates, than ever before. Small businesses partner with others half a continent away to allow both of them to tackle contracts they could never handle alone. Virtual companies operate from inexpensive offices thousands of miles apart. Talk about opportunities for your business!

But this network aids commerce in other ways, too. You can hyperlink shoppers to products at Amazon.com and earn a referral fee. For a fraction of the cost of other advertising, your online store can acquire new customers by means of an affiliate network. New opportunities abound.

■ Opportunity 5.   Segmented Market

Better yet, this vast network called the Internet automatically segments the market into demographic units.

Want to market only to those searching for your particular product or service? Purchase an ad that appears only when someone searches on "life insurance" and you've suddenly begun to strike gold. It's even less expensive to position one of your web pages to come up #3 on an Excite search for the phrase "body surfing" or "sand candles."

If you search Google Groups (http://groups.google.com) for an industry keyword, you'll find e-mail discussion lists and newsgroups populated by just the people you want to reach. Be careful to observe established Netiquette or you'll blow your company's chances for good. But there are your prospects, chatting happily away, a neatly segmented market. Join in the discussion as a fellow learner rather than a salesperson, and you'll begin to attract new business. What an opportunity!

■ Opportunity 6.   Competitive Advantage

One of my friends tells of a phone call from a Japanese businessman a few years ago. "Several of us will visit San Francisco next month," said the caller. "Can we arrange a tour of your world headquarters while we're in the area?"

After my friend had replied, as graciously as he could, that San Francisco was a long way from his city, he walked from his home office to the kitchen. "Dear, there's a group of Japanese businesspeople who want to visit the world headquarters of our company next month."

His wife's face showed panic. "Are they coming here?" she gasped.

No, they didn't come, but ever after this couple shows off to their friends the room they jokingly call "our company's world headquarters."

What I'm describing is the ability of an Internet-savvy businessperson to be every bit as competitive on the Web as a 20- or 200- or 2,000-employee business. It's harder than it used to be. Large companies now budget tens of millions of dollars for their web sites. That's hard to match with a $2,000 to $20,000 small business web site. But it's not impossible to do a very credible job, nevertheless. The market is so huge that even a small slice can generate a quite substantial income for a small business. Opportunities are boundless.

■ Smarts + Sweat + Swiftness = Opportunity

We are years beyond the day when you could slap up a web site and expect the world to beat a path to your door. These days it takes smarts, sweat, and swiftness to compete with the Big Dogs. The opportunity is surely here, but it's not a freebie.

The stupid need not apply. I hear slick salespeople hawking the Internet: "Get your company on the Internet. You don't even have to have a computer." Wrong! To compete on today's Web you must climb a steep learning ladder to discover how to do business. If you can't afford the time to learn how to use the tools, don't waste your money. There are no shortcuts, not even if an infomercial tells you so. That's why you are reading this book on Internet marketing planning. You need smarts.

Sweat is the next ingredient. I get dozens of calls from people who assume that making money on the Internet is easy. Wrong again! Developing a successful business on the Web is just as hard as building a small business in the local strip mall. Oh, the financial investment is much less, but it requires as much work or more. They say that only 20% of new small businesses will celebrate their fifth anniversary. I'm sure this holds true for the Net, as well. The attrition rate is high, partly because people aren't willing to work hard enough to succeed.

Swiftness is the final ingredient. And here is where smaller businesses hold a big advantage. Changing from a strategy that isn't working can take a big company months if not years. It's like turning an ocean liner. But small businesses, like speedboats, can turn quickly and zoom off in a new and promising direction. The environment and business climate on the Web are changing so rapidly that you must be swift-footed to stay in business, see the trends, and be ready to grasp the opportunities as they come. No points are awarded for being late.

The opportunities the Internet offers your business are vast. If you apply smarts, sweat, and swiftness, you can transform these six opportunities into business success.

Exercise: List the kinds of online opportunities that your business can take advantage of.

Chapter 2

Making Your Web Site Purposes Crystal Clear

Over the last several years, many businesses have developed web sites, but most really don't know why. This chapter clarifies your company's purposes for an online presence, which are foundational for effective marketing.

> *"Why, Bunky, do you want a web site?"*
> *"Ah . . . everybody has one and we don't want to look like we're stuck in the Dark Ages."*
> *"So you're concerned about your image?"*
> *"Yeah, image."*
> *"Any other reasons?"*
> *"Well, we want to make money."*
> *"How do you plan to make money on the Web?"*
> *"I'm not really sure."*

Bunky is not alone in his fuzziness and confusion. A great many businesses on the Web find difficulty explaining to someone why they should be on the Internet.

Clarity here can help you develop a lean, clean Internet machine that will accomplish your purposes. Let's look at the five major missions companies seek to accomplish on the Internet: (1) brand development, (2) prospect generation, (3) revenue generation, (4) cost savings, and (5) customer support.

■ Purpose 1. Brand Development

You may have never thought about your company as a brand, so this may be new to you, but stay with me. One of the chief reasons your company has a web site is to demonstrate that you're keeping up with the times, that you're on the cutting edge. You're seeking to communicate an image about your company that will register in the minds of your potential customers. Professional marketers refer to this as brand development.

Your brand is the image of your business in the minds of customers and prospects. Everything about your site—the quality of the design, the clarity of your wording, the sense of interest and excitement, the color scheme, the download time, and much more—contributes to your image, which is your brand identity. Your goal is that when someone leaves your site they'll remember you—positively. And that the next time they come, they'll make a purchase or pick up the phone. Your brand image is also the trust the customer has in you.

There are no real shortcuts here. Major corporations spend millions of dollars to develop their brand image and keep it fresh in the minds of consumers. Is there any way a small business can compete?

Yes, your site can look every bit as good on the Web as a major corporation's, and without spending the big bucks they do. Even though the Web is no longer a level playing field, small businesses can still compete for first impression.

How do I say this without offending you? You need professional help.

Don't get agitated now and reach for your Valium. It's not a shrink I'm talking about, but an experienced web site designer. To compete today you either need to have graphics training and an artistic sense yourself, or you need to hire it. Do-it-yourself will undercut the strong brand identity you are trying to build. Sure, it's cheaper to do it yourself or to have your nephew do it with that spiffy new software he's dying to use on you, but not if it means your business won't get off the ground. Design includes the color scheme and graphics, but also the structure of the site, the all-important navigation system, and the size and quality of the photos or illustrations. All these affect your brand image. Your nephew just doesn't understand brand image yet.

Be very clear about this, whether you are General Motors or a one-person small business, brand development—image—is first on your list of purposes. It is a precondition for sales, since it relates directly to customer trust. Fail at this and you will fail at the core purposes of your site.

■ Purpose 2.   Prospect Generation

In one important business model, you use the Web to bring you leads and provide information to support the sale. Then you close the sale by phone, e-mail, or face-to-face. Many small businesses, especially service businesses, use this model successfully.

My own business is an example. When we were in the web site and online store design business, we used the Web to attract prospects. Our information provided the attraction, then visitors discovered what business we were in and e-mailed or phoned us. A conversation ensued that sometimes resulted in a sale.

A main tool for the prospect generation model businesses is a carefully designed online response form. "Mailto" e-mail links allow people to contact you, but the online form allows you to structure the information people give you so you can qualify the prospect and know how to respond. Some years ago a police products cataloger set up a web site to generate requests for a print catalog. He was astounded at all the internationals who requested a catalog, and found that the people who requested a catalog via his Internet site were more likely to purchase products than the leads he developed from conventional sources—and at a much lower cost. He qualified his leads by asking the name of the organization the inquirer was a member of. It helped him cut down on catalog requests from people who weren't likely to purchase.

If yours is the kind of business where people take a while to come to a decision, or need customized information before they purchase that can only be supplied by a real human being, then prospect generation is probably your main revenue model. This is especially true of products that have a higher price tag or need customization.

You can do a great deal to support the sale, however, by providing a wealth of information online. Sometimes I hear businesspeople protest, "If I tell them everything they need to know, they won't phone me, and I won't be able to complete the sale."

Perhaps. But increasingly, if the prospects don't find the information on your site, they'll surf until they find it on your competitor's site, and then call your competitor instead of you. One of the rules of Internet business is that your competitor is but a click away.

Your online presentation and information should be so complete and compelling that your prospect has no need to leave. I've found that Jesus' saying, "Treat people the way you'd like to be treated," works very well in business. Trust prospects with all the information they need to make a decision, and you increase the chances that they'll trust you with their business.

Be aware, however, that increasingly, companies are finding ways to automate the delivery of customized information, provide quotes via database queries, and then consummate the sale online. Though you may begin with a prospect generation model, you may eventually be forced to adopt an automated system or be crushed by your competition.

■ Purpose 3.   Revenue Generation

The third major goal is revenue generation. Hobby sites don't need to generate revenue. Your company may be putting off revenue generation until they learn the ropes of e-business, or until they generate enough site traffic to produce revenue. But the bottom line for all companies that want to stay in business is revenue generation—somewhere, either offline or online.

For many businesses, revenue generation may seem like the only purpose of a web site. There are three basic ways to generate revenue, which we will consider in detail in the next chapter.

➤ 1.   Sales Transactions

Selling products and services directly over the Web, often referred to as e-commerce, can include a very wide variety, but as a general rule high-ticket items, except commodities, tend to be sold by prospect generation and then personal contact.

➤ 2. Advertising Revenue

If you have enough traffic coming to your site because of your outstanding content then you may be able to sell advertising. The advertising market is depressed currently, however, and you'll probably need other revenue sources to succeed.

➤ 3. Affiliate and Referral Income

A third kind of income is by referrals to other web sites. You could look at it as another form of selling advertising, but since affiliate programs typically pay you only when a sale is actually made, your marketing strategies are quite different. I consider it as a third major source of revenue, though few sites can survive on referral income alone.

■ Purpose 4. Cost Savings

If you like, you might consider the purpose of cost savings as a fourth revenue-generation model. New Internet-only companies may not appreciate the cost savings possible on the Web, but many businesses are able to lower costs significantly by moving essential business processes to the Internet. Ben Franklin recognized this revenue source when he told us, "A penny saved is a penny earned." Let me outline some of the ways that the Internet can save costs.

➤ 1. Staffing

Simply stated, the Internet saves time. It is significantly less expensive—and more accurate—to have a customer enter an order over the Internet than it is to take it by phone or rekey it into your computer system after the sale. In online stores, customers usually wait on themselves, so you don't need as many sales clerks.

However, you will need to increase staffing in other areas—answering e-mail, for example. Since it is so easy to ask questions via e-mail, many more customers are doing so on the Web, overwhelming some businesses. A few react by making it impossible to e-mail them at all (huh?). Others automate their e-mail response systems and provide enough staff to respond to more complex inquiries.

Procurement departments have found that online transactions dramatically cut the cost of processing a purchase order. With the availability of Web-based EDI (Electronic Data Interchange), many smaller businesses are able to conduct B2B (business-to-business) commerce electronically where it was previously cost-prohibitive.

➤ 2. Distribution of Sales Materials

If you've ever run a catalog business, or sent sales materials to your far-flung offices, you know how much money and energy is invested in printing and postage. The Web shines as a way to distribute great amounts of information inexpensively. Many companies put their entire catalog on the Web and then keep it up-to-date, longing for the year when they won't have to print a paper catalog at all. Others put their sales materials on the Internet (or on a company intranet for employees). While there is some expense in converting text and graphics to the Web, once the material is there, it costs next to nothing to keep it there. Updating of data is simpler, too, especially on database-driven sites.

➤ 3. Advertising Costs

For some businesses, especially those in neatly defined niches, advertising costs are lower. Sierra Digital Communications in Rocklin, California, makes microwave radios that transfer data over short distances where trenching and hard-wiring would be cost-prohibitive. Since more and more purchasing agents are using the Web for shopping, and since this is an established product they can search for, advertising costs are low; search engines do much of the work. But most new online businesses seriously underestimate the costs of advertising. People must have a reason to come to your site. If they don't find you by search engines, then you'll need to drive them there by a combination of paid online and offline advertising.

➤ 4. Start-up Costs

When you compare the costs of beginning an Internet business to opening a new brick-and-mortar store, the Web wins hands down.

You can probably think of other ways the Internet saves your company money. But the point is easy to make. One of the purposes of your web site should be saving money. For some businesses this will be more significant than any other purpose.

■ Purpose 5. Customer Support

As Patricia Seybold so eloquently states in her best-selling book, *Customers.com,* successful businesses have this in common: They focus on the customer's needs. This ought to be an important purpose for most business web sites.

Presales support can be enumerated under revenue generation, but postsales support to your customers is a category all of its own. Fortunately, the Web can provide the very best in customer support.

Your system may be as simple as a FAQ or troubleshooting decision tree. What a great way to help your customers! The more material you have, the more valuable a searchable database becomes. Microsoft's site, for example, provides a huge amount of product support information. Epson's site links you to any driver software you may need.

Providing customer support on the Web is not only efficient for the customer, it is also a boon to company customer support departments, who can refer callers to their web site for detailed and complete information, substantially shortening the number and duration of phone calls.

There's no need to be fuzzy about your web site's purposes. Ask yourself these questions:

- How can I present my company in the best possible light? (brand development)
- Can the Internet help us obtain qualified prospects?
- What source(s) of revenue can we realistically expect from our online business?
- How can we achieve maximal cost savings on the Internet?
- How can we provide excellent online customer support?

Answer these five questions and you're well on your way to online success.

Exercise: Write down the main purposes that your web site is seeking to accomplish.

Chapter 3

Devising an Adequate Revenue Plan

Before we get into hardcore planning of your Internet marketing we need to look squarely at revenue sources, since this is foundational to success.

Of the millions of commercial web sites online, only a small percentage have an adequate revenue plan. Most aren't making much money at all. Many are hemorrhaging cash like it was going out of style. Some have already bled to death. But don't fall into the trap of thinking that no one is making money on the Internet. That is simply not true. Tens of thousands of commercial sites are very profitable, and probably hundreds of thousands are making money with the prospect of making more. As the online customer base is building in Europe, Latin America, Asia, and Africa, many more will be able to make money. The key is a clear-sighted revenue plan.

Shoestring businesses can't usually afford the luxury of spending other people's money; small businesses are forced to earn money rather rapidly or not at all—and that's not always a bad thing.

■ Traditional versus E-Businesses

Before we consider revenue strategies, however, I want to acknowledge that many commercial web sites aren't designed to generate revenue themselves, but to increase sales through other channels—and that's an entirely legitimate business plan. An auto dealer, for example, might not transact a car sale over the Internet, but the information on the dealer's site is designed to bring educated prospects into the car lot ready to deal. A manufacturer may offer lots of troubleshooting information and parts lists for product owners, with no online sales at all. Your site may represent your brick-and-mortar business on the Web in order to let customers know you're there and what you offer. That's entirely legitimate.

For several years my site and newsletters were designed to promote my e-commerce site design business. I didn't accept any credit cards at all, but enjoyed a successful and growing business communicating with clients by e-mail, fax, phone, and FedEx. Was that an e-business? Sort of, in that all my advertising and lead generation was done online. But it also had strong similarities to a traditional service business.

> *E-business*—a business designed to generate all or part of its income via the Internet, that is, through services performed or products paid for over the Internet.

In this book, however, I'll be examining e-businesses, which I'll arbitrarily define as businesses designed to generate all or part of their income via the Internet, that is, through services performed or products paid for over the Internet. I agree that this definition may perhaps be a bit narrow, but bear with me for the sake of this discussion. E-businesses look to three primary sources of revenue.

- *Advertising revenue:* Advertisers are paying for exposure on your site or in your e-zine.
- *Referral revenue:* Affiliate programs pay for leads generated, or other types of payment made for performance of one kind or another.
- *Sales transaction revenue:* Income from products or services performed or sold via the Internet.

I'm sure there are some revenue types that don't quite fall under the Big Three, but let's look at each and see their upsides and downsides as sources of revenue for your business.

■ Advertising Revenue

The first common revenue generation model is advertising income from other businesses that want to reach the visitors to your web site.

Many site owners dream of sitting back in their easy chair and letting advertising revenue from their site support them. Few realize this dream. Since the number of commercial web sites is increasing faster than the demand for online advertising, many millions of web pages go without paid advertising, and this tends to drive the cost of advertising down. As dot-com companies have less cash to work with, less is available for advertising. Right now, Internet advertising is in a big slump.

In addition, continual traffic is generated either by continued advertising or by excellent content. But content itself, that is, unique information, illustrations, or entertainment that makes you a destination site, is expensive. Most portals realize that they need multiple streams of revenue in order to prosper, so many are now trying to sell products directly to their visitors as they pass by. Time Warner's Pathfinder site closed because, given its site traffic, an advertising model alone was not sufficient to underwrite the costs of publishing. On the other hand, *Slate* found that charging subscribers cut into their ad revenue (because they had fewer page views). Hence, *Slate* content is now free, and total revenues are said to be higher as a result. Finding the right combination of revenue streams can be difficult.

Advertising revenue is realistic mainly on destination sites that receive a huge amount of web site traffic, and sites narrowly targeted toward customers whom advertisers are willing to pay big bucks to reach.

To see why I say this, let's look at what's happening in Internet advertising. While the average "Rate Card Price" for banner ads has remained steady around $35 CPM (cost per thousand page views), the actual average price at which advertising is selling is substantially lower. You can purchase advertising on numerous ad networks for $5 to $20 CPM for "semi-targeted" ads. That means these ad networks are paying participating web sites about $1 to $10 CPM. Let's see how this works out (see Table 3.1).

Table 3.1   Monthly Revenues

Page Views per Month	Monthly Revenue at $10 CPM	Monthly Revenue at $20 CPM
1,000	$10	$20
10,000	$100	$200
100,000	$1,000	$2,000
1 million	$10,000	$20,000
10 million	$100,000	$200,000
100 million	$1 million	$2 million

3K
30K
300K
3m.

This revenue projection assumes (1) that you sell out your advertising completely each month, and (2) that your costs to sell the advertising allow you to earn a profit. With tens of thousands of web sites there is often unsold inventory available, especially on untargeted sites. To sell advertising you'll need to (1) develop your own in-house sales force, (2) outsource sales to a representative who'll expect 40% to 50% of the gross ad sales, or (3) sell your inventory to an ad network.

Don't confuse ad agencies like Beyond Interactive (www.gobeyond.com) and their staff of media buyers with ad rep agencies such as B2Bworks.com (www.b2bworks.com). Media buyers work on behalf of advertisers, while ad rep agencies work on behalf of web site owners. Ad rep agencies generally don't deal with companies that have fewer than a million or so page views per month, unless these sites are highly targeted.

Let me explain what I mean by targeting. In Table 3.2 you'll see how CPM rates can get very high for a few select categories of web sites. Most, however, fall into the category of untargeted or semi-targeted sites.

Table 3.2 CPM Rates Based on Degree of Targeting

Degree of Targeting	Examples	Approximate CPM
Untargeted	Visitors to a search engine's front page, a portal site, or information site on a general topic such as presidential politics	$1 to $10
Semi-targeted	Teenagers, women, men, sports	$10 to $20
Targeted for higher price goods or services	B2B, small business, golf, investing, health	$25 to $60
Highly targeted	Physicians, attorneys, CEOs	$65 to $100

While advertising used to be a premier revenue source, several trends make it more iffy:

- Advertising dollars are being spent more carefully since the dot-com meltdown on the NASDAQ in spring 2000.
- Sites that carry advertising are getting much more aggressive about selling ads.
- The increase in sites means that inventory (total advertising space available) exceeds paid advertising, and actual sales prices are in decline.
- Media buyers find it easier to deal with a few large ad networks than with dozens of smaller sites.

While advertising can be a substantial revenue source for some sites, you're safer to plan other streams of revenue to supplement it.

■ Referral Revenue—Affiliate Program

If the genius of the Internet is the hyperlink that connects every site in a vast network, then affiliate programs are native-born sons and daughters of the Web.

Referral revenue describes income you receive from referring visitors at your site to another site where they make a purchase, sign up, or take some other kind of action. Sometimes this is called CPA (Cost per Action) or CPC (Cost per Click) advertising. There is a fuzzy line between referral income and advertising. In both cases you are helping to promote another business; you're just getting recompensed in different ways.

One of the most popular types of referral programs is Affiliate (or Associate) Programs. Typically, the site owner (affiliate) signs an agreement with a merchant, or a third-party affiliate service bureau, such as Commission Junction or Be Free, that if someone makes a purchase as a result of clicking on a link at the affiliate site, the affiliate will receive a sales commission of 3% to 15%, and sometimes more.

Alongside affiliate programs I categorize business systems such as www.vStore.com and www.Quixtar.com. They automate the ordering process, but margins are often not enough to allow advertising that will bring significant traffic to the entry page and profit at the end of the month.

Affiliate programs sound like a pretty easy way to make money. No work, just ad a link or a banner and wait for the dollars to roll in. I've belonged to dozens of affiliate programs over the past three years, and have learned this: Affiliate program products must directly relate to the content of your site, preferably integrating the affiliate link into the text of articles and information. Without this close relationship between content and product, your profits are negligible.

High-traffic sites with targeted audiences are required to realize significant income. The right side of each page of my web site is devoted to Web marketing and e-commerce books, many of which I have reviewed. Each is linked to the appropriate product page at Amazon.com. If someone makes a purchase of a book I am directly linked to, I make 15% of the purchase price. If they browse around and find another book, I make 5% of the purchase price. In a recent quarter, for example, here was the report I received from Amazon.com:

Total shipped to customer this quarter:	$14,804.50
Total new customers:	102
Referral fee this quarter:	$1,178.50
Credit referral fee previous quarter:	$0.00
New customer bonus:	$350.00
Total earnings:	$1,528.50

Purchased books from my direct links:

Total shipped: $4,385.87

Referral fee (at 15%): $657.33

Browsed and found books:

Total shipped: $9,877.22

Referral fee (at 5%): $494.10

Other qualifying products:

Total shipped: $541.41

Referral fee (at 5%): $27.07

I share this to point out how much a site with 450,000 page views a month can make on an affiliate program directly related to the content of my site. I also had good success with Ken Evoy's *Make Your Site Sell*! and WebPosition Gold software, and, to a lesser degree, Cory Rudl's *Insider Secrets* course—all very targeted for the interests of visitors who are attracted to my site.

Don't get me wrong. I value the income I receive from affiliate programs. But by themselves, affiliate programs don't make what I consider a good living.

Merchants, however, have found that customer acquisition costs from an affiliate program are substantially less than paying for banner ads with CPM prices. For example, at $35 CPM, a 0.5% click-through rate (the percentage of visitors to a destination site who click on a banner), and a 5% conversion rate (the percentage of visitors to a merchant's site who make a purchase), it would cost a merchant $140 to make a sale. With an affiliate program, the merchant pays only after an actual sale occurs, and the cost per sale is usually 10% or less of the cost of banner advertising. So affiliate programs, or referral programs, are likely to become a major type of advertising for businesses, and site owners will be approached with all kinds of them.

While the monthly income amounts are relatively modest for most site owners, added to other sources of revenue, they can help make a site profitable. Don't expect your small site to support you from affiliate referrals or advertising alone, but consider these as additional revenue streams for your business.

I've reached the conclusion that, for most sites at least, affiliate programs are a good additional source of income, but not a main source of revenue.

■ Sales Transaction Revenue

The third revenue model is completing the actual sales transaction over the Internet. This is often referred to as e-commerce. In spite of all the media hype, only about 5% of retail sales currently take place on the Web. But in a few years I expect that to grow to 20% or more. It will begin to eat into sales at brick-and-mortar stores, and some of those that don't sell online may go out of business.

One of the real promises of the Internet, I believe, is its ability to extend your company's reach beyond your present market area. If you can sell products or services on the Web that can be delivered outside your geographical area, then the world is your marketplace.

Business-to-business e-commerce is growing even faster than online retail; nearly 80% of online transactions are between businesses. While this may not represent new money so much as a new sales channel, it does represent substantial cost savings by reducing transaction costs.

Nirvana for an Internet business is to complete both sales transactions and product delivery over the Web. Entertainment and information sites do this, cutting immensely the staffing and inventory costs for product fulfillment. Industry analysts believe that nearly all software will be delivered over the Internet in the future. Ironically, product fulfillment and delivery are probably where an online business will either rise or fall. With stiff price competition in some industries, the remaining competitive advantage will be how efficiently you can pick, pull, pack, and ship product. Or how cost-effectively you can pay someone else to drop-ship it for you.

While it is much easier now than in 1995 when my company built our first online store for a client, e-commerce is still not simple. Though it is relatively easy these days to set up an online store, that is no guarantee that it will be successful. You must have a number of ingredients in place to make it work effectively and profitably.

Services. I believe that a great deal of revenue will be generated through services sold via the Internet. The services may be performed offline or online, but the ordering and paying for those services will be online. This includes everything from newsletter subscriptions, access to password-protected information, opt-in e-mailing services, tax preparation, database warehousing, and thousands of other services.

The more automated the service, the more "productized" it becomes, and you move from selling time to selling a product. The more person-time invested in performing the service, the closer it is to a regular job. Nevertheless, even though you are selling a time-intensive service over the Internet, you can certainly gather more business through marketing it nationally and internationally.

Products. Hard and soft goods are being bought and sold via the Internet in online stores as well as in eBay, B2B marketplaces, and e-procurement systems in an increasing number of fields. For more than two decades the U.S. economy has supported a thriving mail-order industry. In a sense, an online store is just an automated catalog. But while the Internet automates the front-end ordering process, the make-or-break decisions of the business often rely on the efficiency and costs of back-end product fulfillment and customer service. Drop-shipping is a way of outsourcing inventory, warehousing, and product fulfillment, but it cuts margins and makes it more difficult to offer excellent customer service.

Selling products and services means that you must deal with real customers, some of whom will phone or e-mail you angrily and demand that their concerns be heard. None of this is easy. But I believe that for many site owners, selling or reselling goods and services are the primary ways to make the Internet positively affect the bottom line.

■ Multiple Sources of Revenue

Even better than just one of these approaches is to find ways to incorporate two or even all three sources of revenue in creative and innovative ways. The site that can include advertising revenue, referral revenue, and sales revenue is best positioned to leverage its Internet investments in a way that will produce profits. Make sure that you've designed a realistic plan to bring in the revenue you will need to sustain your Internet business.

Exercise: Identify the sources of income you expect from your online business. Try to quantify the various sources in terms of percentage of total revenue and, if you can, the potential revenue per 1,000 site visitors, or sales, or another metric that you choose. This will help you determine if you have a viable business plan.

Chapter 4

Defining a Unique
E-Business Niche

The key to your online marketing strategy will be recognizing and defining an unfilled or partially filled niche. Here's how to train your eyes.

Standing at the base of the Wailing Wall in Jerusalem and looking up, the immense stone blocks laid one upon another seem to reach to the sky. This most holy site to Jews is all that is left of Herod's Second Temple. It is a place of prayer for the nation. Herod built the Western Wall as part of a retaining wall around the temple mount formed of massive limestone blocks, some weighing over 100 tons each.

But when you look more closely at the Wall, you see the crevices between the massive blocks. In the first two tiers of stone these crevices are filled with papers inscribed with the prayers of the faithful. Above them the crevices are alive: Plants, rooted deeply in the cracks between the stones, abound far above the heads of the worshippers and add character and life to the Wall.

When you move from the sacred to the secular, the Wall

has a lesson for us. If your company doesn't have the mammoth clout of a Fortune 500 corporation, then you must find a niche between the immense players and adapt yourself to thrive there. The English word *niche* comes from a French word that means *to nest*. And that's what small companies can learn to do very successfully, filling small voids left by the big players.

■ Thriving in a Tiny Niche

How can small businesses thrive if the niches seem pretty narrow indeed? You can purchase kitchen knives at Safeway and Kmart, at Macy's and a restaurant supply outlet, as well as in a gourmet cooking store. But a shop that specializes in kitchen cutlery? It would take a major metropolitan area of one or two million people to support such a store, and still it might struggle. But so long as you can deliver your goods or services across distances, on the Internet your marketplace is the nation—and, if you have the vision for it, the world. Some Internet user projections for year-end 2000 are shown in Table 4.1.

A kitchen cutlery shop might die in a town of 10,000 or a city of 100,000. But on the Internet, the market is so huge that even a small slice of the market provides a large number of shoppers. Let's take a country like South Korea, where studies in December 2000 and January 2001 place the number of Internet users as 19 to 20 million, about 42% of the total population. Of these users, 95% report Internet use each week, and half report more than 5 hours per week. Where travel time once prevented shoppers from getting to downtown Seoul's specialty shops, on the Internet the nation is like one very accessible city. With South Korea's 20 million

Table 4.1   Top 15 Nations in Internet Users at Year-end 2000

Rank	Nation	Internet Users (millions)	Share, %
1.	United States	135.7	36.2%
2.	Japan	26.9	7.2%
3.	Germany	19.1	5.1%
4.	United Kingdom	17.9	4.8%
5.	China	15.8	4.2%
6.	Canada	15.2	4.1%
7.	South Korea	14.8	4.0%
8.	Italy	11.6	3.1%
9.	Brazil	10.6	2.8%
10.	France	9.0	2.4%
11.	Australia	8.1	2.2%
12.	Russia	6.6	1.8%
13.	Taiwan	6.5	1.7%
14.	Netherlands	5.4	1.5%
15.	Spain	5.2	1.4%
	Worldwide Total	374.9	

Source: eTForecasts, http://cyberatlas.internet.com/big_picture/geographics/article/0,,5911_151151,00.html

Internet users, even a very narrowly defined specialty business can thrive because of the huge number of potential shoppers. Think of the market as 20 cities of a million people each. That many potential shoppers can support nearly any specialty business.

After six years of intimate involvement with the Internet, I am still awed by its vast potential. To succeed you must be able to see the Internet's hugeness as a market, and at the same time comprehend that even the narrowest kind of business can find enough customers to thrive. The wall is so big that the niches between the huge corporate blocks are quite adequate to support a lively small business marketplace.

■ Differentiating Niches from Blocks

The phone rang and the caller wanted to set up an online store. "I want to sell something on the Internet," he told me.

"What do you plan to sell?" I asked.

"Books," he said, "and consumer electronics."

I can see him competing head-to-head with Amazon, Barnes & Noble, Good Guys, and Best Buy. With his puny resources, he doesn't stand a chance against the big players. None. Nada. Zip.

I've been asked a dozen times, "What would it cost to build a book store just like Amazon.com?" I grind my teeth. With all the opportunities begging to be explored, why would you want to challenge the top dog? I answer that question by saying, "It would cost you the millions and millions of dollars Amazon spent to build its store." Look instead to the niches.

■ The Elusive Holy Grail of the "Ideal" Product

I'm sometimes asked, "What is the best product to sell on the Web?" The answer is pretty straightforward; here are the characteristics:

- Enables a high profit margin
- Offers exclusive sales rights
- Delivers by digital download
- Offers customers more value via Internet sale than through traditional channels
- Fills a universal need
- Must be purchased regularly

If you can score with a majority of those parameters you probably have a winning product or service. But, frankly, few fit. I strongly recommend that you don't let your mind wander aimlessly looking for the perfect product.

A better way is to look to yourself or to your company. (See the following chapter, "Assessing Your Core Competencies.") What are you good at? What do you enjoy? On what subject are you considered the "local world's authority"? What are you strong in? What do you have to offer that is fairly unique? How can you leverage your present strengths? Instead of fantasizing about the "perfect," take what you know and let it empower your vision to see clearly the niches out there.

■ Unfilled Niches

These days it's hard to find a niche that nobody is filling, but occasionally I run across one. The classic path to success is "Find a need and fill it." So look to the customers you know best. What are they asking for? What would they like? What keeps them from fully realizing their own success? Since you're an "expert" in some field, you may have some key insights. You may be able to develop a new or improved product, service, or business process that, coupled with the Internet, can make a big difference. It's your interest and training that give you the vision to see these opportunities. Look closely at the niches.

■ Poorly Filled Niches

While unfilled niches are rare, poorly filled niches are exceedingly common. I've come to expect so much from the

Internet, that I'm often frustrated by what is *not* available online.

Recently I was in the market for a camcorder. I knew practically nothing about them, and I found that the average salesperson at my local stores didn't know much either. I had lots of unanswered questions. I needed information and opinions from people who really knew something about the trade-offs between one recording format and another, but I couldn't find what I was looking for.

There have to be other people like me. What kind of site would make this selection an easier task? The Active Buyer's Guide to Camcorders site was very good, but called on me to make decisions about which I didn't have enough knowledge. Nor did it provide expert opinion or consumer feedback on questions of format pros and cons, answers to my stupid questions, and so on. Amazon's new Camera and Photo Store had a camcorder buying guide, but no individual comments except at the product level. And nothing offered a chart that showed the differences between the models available from a single manufacturer. I was also ready to buy an extra battery pack and a carrying bag, as well as a supply of recording tape, but none of these sites made it easy. I find that Camcorder.com, while good, is a subsidiary of Amdex and Unbeatable.com. They are not really the premium camcorder source; it's only a department in a larger consumer electronics enterprise.

➤ Camcordia.com

I conclude there is no single "greatest place" online to buy camcorders. Maybe I ought to build it myself. In addition to an excellent shopping cart system and checkout procedure, these are the elements I would include:

- Buying guides
- FAQs (frequently asked questions)

- Honest reviews of each manufacturer's product line contrasted with other manufacturers' offerings
- Easy comparisons within a manufacturer's product line
- Live chat that allows shoppers to ask questions from a knowledgeable person 8 to 10 hours per day
- Competitive prices, if not the very lowest
- Carrying all major manufacturers' products
- Inventory of best sellers, drop-ship arrangements for less common requests
- Shipping at a variety of speeds and costs
- A no-quibble guarantee
- Links to product support sections of manufacturers' web sites
- Addresses, phone numbers, and URLs of repair stations
- A full line of accessories
- A full line of recording media
- Information and cables to connect camcorders to TVs, VCRs, and computers
- Online forums where camcorder aficionados discuss detailed questions
- An affiliate relationship with camcorder dealers in regions of the world where I don't want to risk shipping a $250 to $1,500 item.
- A monthly newsletter, *The Camcorder Comrade.*

And I'm sure once I got immersed in the process of building I'd find more to do. We could call it camcordia.com or camcording.net or cambug.com. Isn't this a lot of work? You bet.

(Note: When I first wrote about niches, all my proposed domain names were available. Since then two of the three have been purchased, and camcordia.com has developed a tiny camcorder store, but nothing like the broad vision outlined above.)

Of course, you could build a "good" camcorder store fairly easily, but not an excellent one. Excellence takes high standards, sacrifice, great effort, and a drive to achieve the best you can possibly do. If the project isn't worth doing with excellence, my friends, it probably isn't worth even beginning. Life is too short.

It would probably take six months of work and several thousand dollars to get it fully ready, and a year or two to get it functioning at full potential. Is it possible? Of course! Would it succeed? I have no doubt! Am I going to build it? No. This one needs someone who lives and breathes camcorders. But camcorders are a poorly filled niche just begging to be filled with excellence.

■ Partly Filled Niches

I've often toyed with the idea of setting up a firm that helps small businesses market their web sites. One that considers each company's needs carefully and recommends a marketing plan tailored to each company's needs and budget. One that offers exceptional value and a personal touch. One that doesn't rest until the customer's need has been fully addressed. Aren't there plenty of firms that specialize in online marketing already? Yes, indeed. But I believe I could make one succeed, since there are hundreds of thousands of small business web site entrepreneurs out there, and only ten or twenty thousand marketing companies, many of which aren't very effective at all with small businesses. Many excellent businesses exist, such as Webster Group International (www.wgi.com) but there is a tremendous need still. Do I plan to do this? No, but it could be done quite profitably. This is a partly filled niche longing to be filled more completely.

■ Creating New Niches

We haven't nearly exhausted the subject of niches yet. How about creating a new niche where one didn't exist before? I love what JustBalls.com (www.justballs.com) did when they began in 1998. They didn't pump themselves up to think they could tackle the whole sporting goods sector. They weren't a

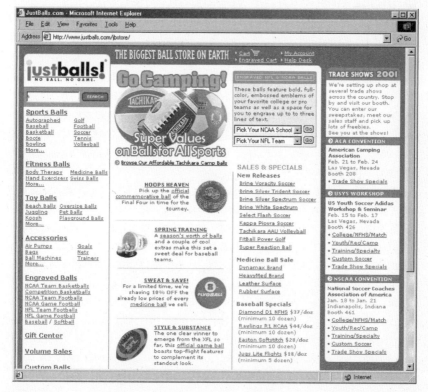

Figure 4.1 JustBalls.com (Copyright © 1998–2001, Justballs, Inc. All rights reserved.)

Big 5 or a FogDog. So they sliced sporting goods in a way that it had never been sliced before—balls only. They don't sell bats and first-baseman's mitts. They sell balls. Baseballs, basketballs, footballs, golf balls. If it's a sports ball of any kind, they have it. Now they offer laser-engraved sports balls for gifts and presentations. Several years later they are still in business because they created a brand-new niche, found a catchy, memorable name, developed a customer-centered approach, and opened their doors. See Figure 4.1.

■ Brick-and-Mortar versus Internet Niches

I need to say a word to you who have an existing brick-and-mortar business already. Should you put your business on the Web? By all means, do so! (Unless you're a barber, or something inescapably local, of course.) The stability of your traditional business will give you the time to find your way online. But don't put your entire business offerings online, only those that are unique and especially adaptable to the Internet.

Several years ago, Jeff Greene called me for help setting up an online store. Jeff is the longtime owner of The Office Market, a traditional office and art supplies store in Conway, New Hampshire, an area of about 20,000 people in the White Mountains. This was before OfficeDepot.com, OfficeMax.com, and Staples.com had developed a strong presence online. He asked me if he should sell both office supplies and art supplies. I pointed him toward the niche market and away from the mass market, and he has since done well with Discount Art Supplies (www.discountart.com) offering a full line of top-brand, high-quality brushes, paints, and other supplies. If Jeff had tried to put his whole office supply inventory online, the e-business would have lost focus and he wouldn't have been able to carry a full enough line to compete with the big companies (though in his local region The Office Market is the leader). By putting all his energy into the art supplies part of his business, he has succeeded admirably on the Web and he can compete with others in this field. See Figure 4.2.

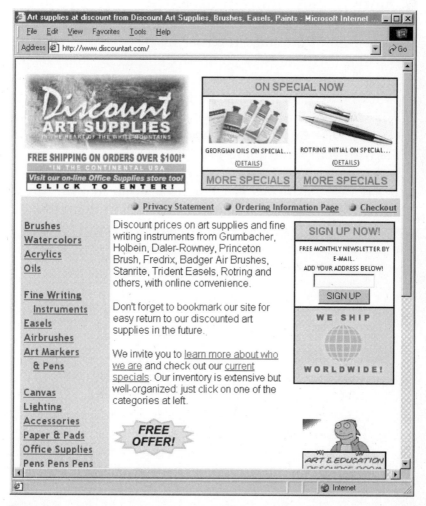

Figure 4.2   Discountart.com (Copyright © 2001 Discount Art Supplies. Used by permission.)

Determine what aspect of your current business is best for the Internet and put that online; don't load your web site with generic products and services that diffuse your focus.

■ Finding and Filling Your Niche

The promise of the huge Internet market is there for you, too. While it is intensely competitive, the size and lack of geographical barriers are especially suited to small business-people who are blessed with niche vision and a dose of creativity and determination. Look closely, now—not at the massive blocks but at the niches between them—and find niche with your name on it.

Exercise: List the niches you might be interested in filling. Next, assess the quality of the existing sites in those niches. Now list the unfilled, underfilled, and partially filled niches you can identify.

Chapter 5

Assessing Your Core Competencies

The first question you ask yourself isn't "How can I make a million dollars on the Internet?" The question should be "What am I good at?" That's where your business begins.

I'm frequently asked, "How can I make money on the Internet?" That's the wrong question. A better question is, "What am I good at?" Existing companies need to ask the question, too. What are *we* good at? What are our core competencies? And how can we leverage those competencies into a viable online business?

You don't get something for nothing. There is no affiliate program that can make you wealthy without offering value to your web site visitors. You must offer value, and that value is closely related to your core competencies. This may sound elementary—and it is—but many e-businesses start up without being able to offer value and then wonder why they don't succeed. This is a business question, but it is also a marketing question. If you're going to design a marketing plan, you first need to know what your competitive advantage is, and that flows directly from what you're good at.

■ Identify Your Interests, Abilities, and Strengths

If you have a one-person business, start with jobs you've held. Is there anything you're well versed in? Do you know a trade or an industry well? Do you have a hobby that you've become an expert in?

If you are a larger business, what do you do the very best? Not your corporate hype, but what you really excel at. You may have the very best such-and-such in your industry. Perhaps you've won awards in a certain area. What are your core competencies?

A strong e-business—any business, for that matter—is founded upon excellence. If there is no area in which you have achieved excellence, I really don't recommend starting a business. Life is too short to fail one more time.

Are you great at manufacturing a quality, useful product? Can you provide a needed service flawlessly and evoke customer delight time after time? Are you good at logistics, managing the flow of products? Do you possess great knowledge about racing bicycles? Look for areas of competence, of excellence. That's the bedrock of your business.

■ Identify Your Passions

You may be very good at what you do but hate every minute of it. Not likely, though. We usually hate those things we fumble with or fail at. The point is, you must have a passion for your business activity if you're going to succeed. Without it, you won't last. You won't put in the long hours required if you don't like it. You'll put off doing what you need to do now. And passion without competence won't make it, either. But excellence combined with enthusiasm is a winning combination.

■ Identify Your Competitive Advantage

Like it or not, when you put your business on the Web to offer products or services nationally or internationally, you are in competition. If you simply have a brochureware page for your Mercedes repair business in Centerville, you probably don't have many competitors; your market is defined by how far people are willing to travel to get their Mercedes repaired. But if you decide to sell Mercedes accessories or add-ons, repair manuals, photo books, or replacement hood ornaments online, you've just entered the competitive arena. You've just launched a business that will compete for sales internationally.

To succeed, you need to identify your set of core competencies. Determine what kinds of competencies your online competitors bring to the Web, and then see how to leverage your strengths to gain a competitive advantage. There is little need for 15 Mercedes accessory web sites located in the United States. A few will succeed, and the rest will get so little business that they'll drop off the Web in a year or two. To succeed you need to find a way to leverage your strengths so that you can offer something better than your competition— better selection, better service, better prices, more interesting photos and articles, and a larger collection of used Mercedes hood ornaments. Something must be better or you'll fail to attract attention and repeat buyers. Mediocrity leads to bankruptcy.

■ Decide How to Sustain Your Competitive Advantage

Finally, you'll need to determine how to maintain your competitive advantage over time. In any business, but especially on the Web, innovations can be copied easily. Your great idea that pulls you ahead of your competition will be reproduced. Amazon.com began the Internet's first affiliate program, but BarnesAndNoble.com soon was working to develop its own affiliate network and encourage its affiliates to market through the signatures in their e-mail messages.

You may have a unique expertise or strength, but can you sustain that over the long haul? An idea may rocket you ahead for a while, but a pattern of innovation is necessary to keep you ahead. Successful businesses count their people and in-house expertise as their most valuable assets. You'll need to retain your cutting-edge competence in order to make future gains on the Web.

So what determines the shape of your online business? Your core competencies, your areas of excellence. Determining what they are, and engaging them in building your e-business, is a crucial step in developing an online marketing plan.

Exercise: List your company's main core competencies. Determine how they will shape the direction of your business. Decide what core competencies are necessary to acquire in order to be competitive in the direction you choose. Begin to write these down and keep notes on your reflections. This may take a while to come together, but get started now.

Chapter 6

Developing a Unique Sales Proposition (USP)

The biggest problem with e-business I see is not flaky web pages, but businesses that haven't differentiated themselves from their competitors. Here's why this is vital, and how to do it.

To succeed in the heavily populated world of Internet businesses, you need to know exactly what your business is and what differentiates it from all other online businesses. You need to develop a *Unique Selling Proposition,* a USP.

When I go to e-commerce trade shows, if I had a nickel for every time I see the phrase "e-commerce solutions," I'd be a rich man. So you have a solution. A solution to what? If 20 other companies offer an e-commerce solution, why should I do business with *your* firm? Unless you have a ready answer to that question, your days in business are numbered. You *must* know what makes you different, better, or more capable than your competition.

■ What Is a Unique Selling Proposition?

A Unique Selling Proposition (USP) is a brief one- or two-sentence statement that clearly, concisely, and compellingly states the unique strengths and vision that your company or product bring to the marketplace.

The name should evolve naturally from your niche. As I was reading Dan Janal's e-book *Branding on the Internet* (Aesop, 2000; www.brandingthenet.com), I came across a wonderfully simple positioning exercise which Janal calls his "Fool Proof Positioning Statement." It is an extremely useful fill-in-the-blanks approach. First, you need to decide what to put in the blanks (see Table 6.1).

Table 6.1   Janal's Fool Proof Positioning Statement

Elements of Your Positioning Sentences	Example
Name of the company or product (insert your tentative company name here)	Acme Ceiling Grip
Category	sheetrock screw
Core audience	contractors
Key benefit	attach sheetrock ceilings more securely
Key differentiating feature	doesn't rust when wet

Let's fill in the blanks of the first sentence:

(Name) is a *(Category)* that helps *(Core audience)* achieve *(Key benefit)*. "Acme Ceiling Grip is a sheetrock screw that helps contractors attach sheetrock ceilings more securely."

While the first sentence helps you state the benefit clearly, the second sentence helps you differentiate yourself from competitors:

Unlike other (Category), (Company name or product) has (Key differentiating feature). "Unlike other sheet-rock screws, Acme Ceiling Grip doesn't rust when wet."

This may seem simplistic, but take a couple of minutes right now to see the power of it for your own online company. You might want to stress different key benefits to other core audiences, but this will give you a start. Keep working on your two or three sentences until they are clear and compelling.

Sometimes the term "Unique Selling Proposition" is criticized in that it is merchant-centric rather than customer-centric, that it should be termed a "Unique *Buying* Proposition." Of course, it should be stated from the customer's viewpoint, but there's no need to change the term.

Whatever you call it, having a short, snappy, strong sentence or two to describe what you offer uniquely will make the difference between success or failure for your online company.

■ Examples of USPs

Since this is such an important concept, let me give you a few examples from my own web sites.

JesusWalk.com (www.jesuswalk.com) provides e-mail lessons and discussion groups to help participants learn over time what Jesus said and did, and how to live as his modern-day disciples. JesusWalk is staffed by volunteers and supported by donations from participants.

Doctor Ebiz (www.doctorebiz.com) takes real questions from real small businesspeople and provides brief no-nonsense answers that help them learn how to succeed in the online world. Doctor Ebiz is advertising supported and distributed via e-mail subscription, web site, web site syndication, and newspaper syndication.

Struggling to market your company on the Web? You've come to the right place! Wilson Internet (www.wilsonweb .com) offers the Web's largest source of key information about doing business on the Net—hundreds of articles, thousands of links to resources on e-commerce and Web marketing. (Note: This web site USP begins with a problem to be solved and states the solution.)

There are a number of formats you can use to state a USP. But getting it down on paper is a crucial marketing move. USPs that float too long in the cranium may not be sharp or concise enough to communicate clearly to others. Write it down! Then consider using part or all of it on your web site first page. It should be that compelling!

➤ Amphibious Case Study

Just for fun, we're going to develop a USP for a new dot-com start-up. Let's say you've looked deep into yourself for your areas of expertise and all you can find is that you love amphibians. Ever since you were a kid, you've taken in frogs and toads as pets. You developed the first salamanderia in your local town zoo. You have nearly every book ever published on amphibians, and you subscribe to the scientific journals that carry amphibian research. You love amphibians!

➤ Examine the Competition

You scour the Web looking for amphibian sites. I looked up the word "amphibian" to see what I could find.

Kingsnake.com. "The information portal for the reptile and amphibian hobbyist." It has links to various nature magazines, discussion groups, etc. (www.kingsnake.com).

Amphibians discussion list. Dedicated to the distribution of knowledge, care, and breeding of all amphibians. This is where you'll find many of your potential customers (http://groups.yahoo.com/group/amphibians/messages).

Big Apple Herpetological. Reptile and amphibian supplies. They claim to be "the Universe's Largest Selection of Reptile & Amphibian Supplies" with over 750 quality products. They offer same-day/next-day shipping, full product consultation, and the guaranteed lowest prices (www.bigappleherp.com). (See the USP stated clearly in their brief ad?)

The Herp Mall. Provides Web services for various herp (reptiles, amphibians, arachnids, chelonians, etc.) dealers, supply dealers, and event coordinators. They claim 25,000 visitors per day. Here's where you can advertise (www.herp.com).

There are also numbers of local reptile and amphibian societies.

➤ Where's the Gap?

One thing became pretty clear as I searched for amphibian businesses. While reptiles are well serviced on the Web, amphibians are left out, second best. Most sites tilt toward reptiles. Could you become *the* commercial amphibian site on the Net? There's a gap online. The only question I have is whether or not the market is large enough to support an online business focusing primarily on amphibians.

With this narrow a niche, I doubt that you'll have many

amphibian product advertisers clamoring for space in your advertising calendar, so you'll need to look for revenue streams primarily in product sales.

➤ What's the Name?

Why don't you go to Network Solutions' Whois Database (www.networksolutions.com/cgi-bin/whois/whois) and see what's available? A number of names are taken, but I could still find some good ones left when this was written: WartyToad.com, FrogLover.com, and NewtBabe.com. You could probably find others. But I like FrogLover.com. (It has since been taken.) Yes, AmphibianLover.com is available, but it doesn't have the ring of truth, the same kind of rhythm as FrogLover.com. We'll talk more about naming in the chapter entitled "Naming Your Online Business."

➤ A USP to Fill the Gap

Now let's formulate a USP that fills the gap we've observed in the online amphibian world:

> *"FrogLover.com is your destination shop for amphibians: supplies, books, information, research, and gossip—the most comprehensive amphibian site on the Web."*

Your Unique Selling Proposition differentiates you from any of your competitors. Armed with a strong USP you can develop a Web business that doesn't have *any* direct competitors. You're on your way.

Exercise: Write the first draft of a USP for your business. Then study two of your chief competitors and write a USP describing them. Now review and rewrite your USP in light of what you've learned.

Chapter 7

Setting Goals for Your E-Business

Just what do you expect to get out of your e-business this year? Or over the next several years? Setting some realistic goals is a crucial step.

An important strategic marketing planning step is a brief look at goal clarification. What do you expect to get out of your e-business this year? Or over the next several years? Your goals, of course, are intimately related to every other aspect of your business plan. You'll want to massage your goals again and again as you research various aspects of your marketing plan. But let's start somewhere.

First of all, let's define terms. By goal or objective I mean a clear, numerical, time-quantified statement of what your expectations are. This shouldn't be fuzzy, such as: "to learn about e-commerce and have a good time in the process, while making adequate money." Let's be crystal clear. Goals ought to be both financial and nonfinancial and related to the length of your marketing plan's timeline. Let me illustrate:

Nonfinancial Goals:

- To grow steadily in market share each year from our current 13% to 32% over five years.

- To grow the sales from our store's web site from 5% to 45% of total sales over five years.

- Using cultural and language translations of our web site, to open up markets for our line of men's polo shirts in the major European languages and in 12 countries in Western Europe. Beginning with Spanish in year one and Portuguese in year two, followed by French, Italian, German, and others.

- Use cultural adaptations of our Spanish language site in year two to open markets in Mexico, Central America, and key South American countries. In year three, adapt our European Portuguese site to penetrate Brazil.

- To introduce our polo shirt line in the four major Western U.S. department store chains, two of the chains in the first 18 months.

- Just because your business is much smaller than our polo shirt example doesn't mean you shouldn't be setting measurable goals. Your goals will be much more modest, but no less important, such as "Move from hobby site to a profit center within two years. Year one, add e-commerce capability. Year two, develop advertising revenue from both web site and e-mail newsletters."

- Increase the number of visitors and page views from 6,000 and 18,000 per month to 20,000 and 60,000, respectively, over a period of six months, using a combination of traffic-producing strategies.

- Redesign the site over the next eight months using professional graphics, e-commerce, and webmaster contractors to make the site visually attractive and easy to maintain.

Financial Goals:

- To grow annual sales from $2.3 million in 2002 to $6.8 million by the end of 2004.

- To obtain a first-round venture capital investment in 18 months in the range of $2 million.

- Build gross site revenue to $7,500 by June of 2002, and to $47,000 by June of 2003.

Goals have a way of stretching us, giving us direction when we've lost perspective, and driving us to do our best. They're a vital part of your Internet Marketing Plan.

Exercise: Develop at least five nonfinancial and financial goals for your business. Expect to change them a number of times over the next several weeks. But put *something* on paper today.

Part II
Situation Analysis

I consult with dozens of companies and correspond with owners and marketing managers of many more. One of the most serious weaknesses I see is a blindness in marketing managers or owners to what is going on around them. To succeed we must take time to understand the rapidly changing situation in which we find the Internet market at a given point in time. Here are some tools to help you lay the knowledge groundwork that underlies your Internet Marketing Plan.

Chapter

Performing a SWOT Analysis

This is a handy tool to quickly get the big picture of your company's strengths, weaknesses, opportunities, and threats.

Restaurants ought to make bigger paper napkins since some of the most productive business ideas seem to come to mind over a meal. The SWOT (Strengths, Weaknesses, Opportunities, Threats) analysis technique (see Table 8.1) lends itself to napkin planning and snapshot insights. To conduct a SWOT analysis, draw a vertical line in the center of your napkin (or whiteboard or flipchart), intersected by a horizontal line. Now you have four quadrants where you'll sketch your company's situation.

Table 8.1 The SWOT Analysis Technique	
Strengths	**Weaknesses**
Opportunities	**Threats**

Though a great deal of research may lie behind what's in each box, keep what you write down simple and incisive. Collecting these facts and ideas together in one place energizes you to see the big picture. Use it as a brainstorming tool, a strategy formation tool. Note that the first pair of categories—strengths and weaknesses—refers to your company's *internal* nature, while the second pair of categories refers to *external* opportunities and threats.

■ Strengths

In the first box, list all the strengths your company possesses. Don't be modest. Spell them out. If you perform this with other people, you might begin by brainstorming words that characterize your company and writing them down as fast as people say them. Then use those ideas to construct a profile of your company's strengths.

■ Weaknesses

In the second box list weaknesses, areas your business lacks or doesn't have the personnel to cover well. Be honest. It's better to face the bad news now than construct an unrealistic marketing plan that is doomed to failure.

■ Opportunities

The third box is for opportunities. When you look at the market (and we're looking particularly at the Internet market in this book), what do you see? What aren't your competitors doing that customers need? Look for gaps. (Of course, ana-lyzing your competitors is called a competitive analysis; none of these elements of a marketing plan stand alone; they're all interrelated.) Get down the basics here. Gaps may not last long. What you see as an opportunity today may not exist in three months. A SWOT analysis is only a snapshot in time, not a permanent document.

■ Threats

The final box is for threats to your business. What trends do you see that could wipe you out or make your service or product obsolete? What are your competitors doing to push themselves ahead? What new dot-com start-up is trying to move into the market?

Table 8.2 shows an example of how a SWOT analysis might look for an imaginary animal greeting card site, CrawlyCards .com, specializing in pictures of ground-clinging creatures such as slugs, snails, and puppy dog tails.

Obviously this company has a real problem—no effective revenue model—but at least it's looking at alternatives. This is what a SWOT analysis can do for you, and may be the germ of an idea that will revolutionize the snail and slug card business as we know it.

(To those of you from a different culture, this example is a joke. Please don't take it seriously; it's just an example of Yankee poor taste. It helps lighten up an otherwise dull subject.)

Exercise: Prepare a SWOT chart for your business using the blank form supplied here. It will help you assess what you do and don't do well, what you need to be careful of, and how you can improve.

Table 8.2 A SWOT Analysis for a Greeting Card Site

Strengths	Weaknesses
Unique idea, no one else is even close.	Small opt-in customer list, most site usersseek to remain anonymous.
Strong artistic team includes some of the finest slug and insect illustrators in the country.	Few advertisers interested in this strangely targeted market.
Excellent animation abilities.	Perl script that runs the site is slow and needs to be rewritten in a compiled language.
Source of inspirational card inscriptions for all occasions.	Lack of interest from venture capitalists.
Experienced and innovative company officers.	Single stream of revenue is advertising, and that is slim pickin's.

Opportunities	Threats
No real competitors in our precise space.	Chemical companies are producing more effective snail bait that may destroy gastropod populations in our lifetime.
Much traffic from students at UC Santa Cruz (Banana Slug is their mascot) sending cards each other. Possible joint venture with alumni association and the *Official Pacific Northwest Slug Page* (www.tammyslug.com).	Large card sites such as Blue Mountain (www.bluemountain .com) might want to take over the slug and mollusk traffic and edge us out.
Advertising from French restaurants and their suppliers.	
Possible book sales such as: *Slugs and Snails* (*Minipets*), *Field Guide to the Slug,* and *Creepy Crawly Cuisine: The Gourmet Guide to Edible Insects.*	
Possible sales of Turbo Snails to browse algae in fish tanks.	
Partnership with CyberSlug Adoption Center.	
E-commerce venture selling scarab jewelry; possible advertisers among pet supply and fish supply stores, bug jewelry manufacturers.	
Possible affiliate program with snail bait companies.	
Possible cross promotion with Conchologists of America.	

Strengths	Weaknesses

Opportunities	Threats

Chapter 9

Conducting
an Industry Analysis

In the planning phase it's wise to analyze industry trends so you can position your company ahead of the curve rather than behind it.

As you create your Internet Marketing Plan, you must develop an industry analysis—develop a grasp of where your particular industry seems to be going and the trends that are taking place so you can position your company ahead of the curve rather than behind it.

■ Trade Journals

It's hard to tell where you'll find an existing analysis of your industry. Start with the dominant trade journals for your particular industry. How do their columnists and analysts see the online future for the industry? Look especially at the first issue of the new year when pundits are called upon to pundicate about the future. Try to include some statistics about the size of the market in your industry, the quantity of goods and services sold on and off the Internet, and projections for future sales. Unfortunately, some trade journals just haven't moved into the Internet age. They feel deeply threatened by the Internet and don't understand it yet.

■ Investment Industry

A second place to look is the investment industry. Teams of researchers working for brokerage houses and information services comb various sectors looking for stocks to recommend to their clients. Since lots of money is involved, the research is careful, and insights can often be rewarding. Also check magazines such as *Fortune* (www.fortune.com), *Forbes* (www.forbes.com), *Red Herring* (www.redherring.com), and *Upside* (www.upside.com).

■ Internet Analysis

For a specifically Internet perspective on various industries, read *The Standard* (www.thestandard.com; the print version is known as *The Industry Standard*), *E-Commerce Times* (www.ecommercetimes.com), and *Iconocast* newsletter (www.iconocast.com). I also read Dana Blankenhorn's insights in *ClickZ* (www.clickz.com) and *A-Clue.com* (www.a-clue.com). Firms specializing in Internet research sometimes analyze whole industries—and hope to sell you the report. One leader is Forrester Research (www.forrester.com). The E-Commerce Research Room at WilsonWeb.com (www.wilsonweb.com/research) scours the Web for such analyses in many sectors.

It's difficult to be exhaustive since the literature is mush-rooming, but it's a great starting place. It pays to read widely, looking for nuggets of online strategies found successful in other industries that could be translated into your own.

Once you've done your research, summarize in a few points the trends you see. You don't want to write a lot, just enough to clarify current directions to show that your strategies are working with the direction of industry trends rather than at cross-purposes or lagging behind.

Exercise: Create a short list of the four or five trends that seem to be driving change in your industry. Then write one or two sentences that state how your company is taking advantage of or adjusting to these trends.

Example: The construction materials industry is facing a shortage of some materials, such as wood products, and a shortage of skilled workers. Acme Building Supply's online business meets these needs by helping our visitors find lumber sources for scarce products and providing a bulletin board where both employers and employees can post job openings or position-wanted ads.

Chapter 10

Analyzing the Competition

While you don't want to obsess over your competition, you'd better know how you are positioned vis-à-vis other businesses in your space. Here are some tips.

One serious error I see too often is blindly going online with a "successful" business plan pioneered by an earlier online competitor. Why are many so-called portal sites still springing up?! Enough already! In many cases, established competitors are so strong that the new business has no chance of success. Internet business space is extremely crowded—mostly by smaller players. You've *got* to understand the competition if you want to devise a successful Internet Marketing Plan. Your goal is to identify your company's chief competitors, analyze their individual marketing strategies, and see where to position your company.

■ Identify the Leaders

The first step is to identify the major players. Start with the Yahoo! Directory category or categories closest to your business. While the Yahoo! Directory (www.yahoo.com) is no longer comprehensive, it will list the major players. Print out the directory for your category, and then research every link, making notes on your printed copy. Look for the larger companies, innovative approaches, new products, and so forth.

You can often see which companies get the most traffic by checking Media Metrix 500 (www.mediametrix.com). You can also learn about traffic levels by using Alexa (www.alexa.com); a free add-on to your web browser, it ranks the traffic to each site you visit in terms of Top 100, Top 1000, Top 10,000, etc., giving you a rough idea of your competitors' positions in the traffic pecking order.

■ Scrutinize the Leaders

The second step is to study the top 5 or 10 competitors carefully. You can learn a lot from their web sites. Make notes on what you discover. Look for:

- Products or services offered. Note especially any that differ from your own offering.
- What is the distribution system for products: inventory, distributor, drop-shipping, download?
- Customer service. Look for guarantees, policies, procedures.
- Look, feel, and functionality of the web site.
- Capability and personalization of the shopping cart/ sales system.

- Advertising campaigns and offers.
- Strengths and weaknesses from the customer's point of view, not yours.
- Strategies and objectives.
- Statement of vision or purpose, or what amounts to a Unique Selling Proposition on the site.
- Areas where the competitor holds a market advantage.
- Vulnerabilities or gaps in what is offered.

If the company is publicly traded, you can learn more under SEC filings at Edgar Online (www.edgar-online.com) and a variety of investment information services. Write down the names of key officers and look for interviews or speeches that will give you clues.

■ Highlight Strengths, Vulnerabilities, and Gaps

Third, summarize your findings into a sentence or two highlighting key strengths and weaknesses you find for each top competitor. If this is an especially imposing competitor, note strategies necessary to counter their offering. Your strategies may vary depending upon your own strengths. If you have a large cash reserve, for example, you might want to blow away the competition by vastly outspending them in effective advertising. But if you're small, you'll need to use your ingenuity to leverage your strengths to take advantage of your competitors' weaknesses.

Though the accumulated research for this section of your Internet Marketing Plan may be voluminous, distill it down to a few paragraphs that capsulize your competitors and how you plan to deal with them. What you may decide after surveying the competition is that the field is too crowded, and you don't have anything particular to offer that your competitors don't. Perhaps your decision should be to tailor your online offerings to areas in which you *can* compete successfully, or decide not to compete at all.

I see far too many copycat sites trying to compete gamely for the same space. They can't all survive competing head-to-head. The smaller sites must find a niche in which they can flourish or be driven out of business. Don't put up a web site just to do it; don't waste your time and money unless you have a plan to carve out a profitable business on the Web despite the competition.

But don't be frightened away prematurely, either. Remember David and Goliath. The larger the company, the more slowly it makes decisions and the more the officers are interested in retaining their own jobs rather than risking security to gain a competitive advantage. You *can* find weaknesses and gaps if you look carefully for them. Then use your ingenuity to offer the customer more than he or she can find anywhere else.

Exercise: List your 10 top online competitors and explain how you are differentiating your business from theirs.

Chapter 11

Understanding
Your Customers

Here are some of the important factors to consider when learning about your customers. The better you know them, the more effectively you can market to them.

A surefire formula for success is to understand thoroughly who your customers or clients are, and what they are looking for. It's easy to rely on assumptions. But when you begin a serious study of your customers, your chances of success go way up.

■ Preparing a Customer Profile

If yours is an existing company, then you probably have a pretty good idea of what your best customers look like. But when you move your business online, the profile of your customers may change. Likely you are moving from a local or regional business to a national business. Now you're attracting customers in a different way than you have in the past. If

you're planning a new online start-up, it is especially important to define your customers.

> *Consultant:* You've got a new breed of African violets to
> sell, Melissa. Who do you plan to sell them to?
>
> *Melissa:* Oh, everyone will be excited about the new
> colors and characteristics of our plants. I
> think everyone will want one.
>
> *Consultant:* That's not too helpful. Who will be most
> interested, do you think?
>
> *Melissa:* I'll get my best response from people who
> are members of the African Violet Society of
> America, I would guess.
>
> *Consultant:* Tell me about these people. Do you ever go to
> any of their local events?
>
> *Melissa:* Yes, I attended two all-day workshops in town
> last year. They were fabulous.
>
> *Consultant:* Tell me about the participants. Were they pri-
> marily men or women? What age group did
> they seem to be? How did they dress? What
> kinds of cars were in the parking lot? Did
> any children come with them? What per-
> centage was on the Internet? What races
> were represented? Did you detect anyone
> speaking with a foreign accent? What coun-
> try were they from? Which regional branch
> of the African Violet Society seems to be the
> strongest?

You're beginning to get the picture. When you're looking
at everyone as potential customers, you miss your best customers. Sure, you'll get a scattering of people who don't fit
your profile, but you need to aim your marketing at a carefully defined group of people. Or maybe you'll find that
there are two or perhaps three separate kinds of people you
can define who are best customers.

As part of developing your Internet Marketing Plan, you need to carefully define these people. Everything flows from who your customers are: your web site design, your product or service offerings, your modes of advertising. Everything!

■ Learning about Your Site Visitors

You can learn about your site visitors in a number of ways. But before we look at any of them, we need to talk about privacy. One of your visitors' chief concerns is the steady erosion of their privacy. If you want to gather information, you'll need to show integrity about the way you use the information. I strongly recommend that you develop a site privacy policy, link to it from every form (and preferably from every page in your site), and abide by it rigorously. Why don't you read our privacy policy (www.wilsonweb.com/clients/privacy-policy.htm), and then, if you don't already have one, use information at the Direct Marketing Association site to develop your own (www.the-dma.org/library/privacy). There are eight ways you can learn about your site visitors:

➤ 1. Monitor E-Mail Inquiries and Complaints

It's vital that you find a way to monitor e-mail inquiries and complaints from your site visitors. Even if you have an employee handle this e-mail for you, have him or her print out an extract of key questions and complaints so you can keep your finger on the pulse. I've found that my blind sides are quickly spotted by visitors who'll fire off an e-mail. Don't look at these e-mails as enemy fire; these are your friends who'll help you improve your site. When you spot a question occurring again and again, it's a sign that you need to deal with it more fully or more visibly on your site. And it tells you what is important to your visitors.

➤ 2. Provide Online Questionnaires

You might want to create an online questionnaire with which you can gather information from your site visitors. What kinds of questions are important? The *Internet World* subscription form is an example of questions asked by a Business-to-Business magazine (http://subscribe.penton.com/inw) to provide information of interest to advertisers. I've developed demographic surveys for two of my sites:

> Web Marketing Today survey assumes a business-to-business readership (www.wilsonweb.com/survey).

> Christian Articles Archives survey looks at individual financial data as well as purchasing authority in a nonprofit organization setting (www.joyfulheart.com/admin/wmt-sample.htm).

Each of these questionnaires is limited to 12 questions, assures anonymity, and displays a privacy policy link. I also use surveys to evaluate each Bible study series I conduct in order to learn what participants like and don't like. This way I am able to continually improve.

Yes/no and multiple-choice answers are especially easy to analyze, though fill-in-the-blank questions may give you some vital information you won't get otherwise. Your visitors will need some incentive to fill out your survey or questionnaire. Perhaps your incentive will be information, entry in a contest, or a free prize. I sometimes ask visitors to answer demographic questions after filling out a contact form or subscribing to my newsletter. After enough people have completed the survey, I'll typically download the data file, import it into Microsoft Access or Excel, and conduct an analysis using queries or cross-tabs, and graphing.

An increasing number of companies are offering survey services online. I've developed a partial list of these for your use (www.wilsonweb.com/wmt5/web-surveys.htm). One of the easiest to use is Zoomerang (www.zoomerang.com).

➤ 3. Send Out E-Mail Questionnaires

The strength of online forms is the ease with which the data can be collected for analysis. The downside is that online forms are essentially passive; they wait until someone comes to them. E-mail questionnaires, on the other hand, are active. They come directly to your selected participant.

Text e-mail questionnaires can be difficult to analyze quickly. A special program must be developed to harvest information from fields delimited by brackets or some other symbol. If the recipient places an answer outside of the brackets, or gives the wrong kind of answer, the survey may have to be discarded or manually scored. E-mail questionnaires, however, may be the survey of choice because of their immediacy and ease in sending. I got a nearly 50% response from a recent survey to newsletter readers. That's pretty good!

In early 2001, most Internet users' e-mail programs now support HTML e-mail forms. I've had good success at constructing an HTML form and sent it out via e-mail. Recipients click on check-boxes or fill out answers. When they click on the Submit button it automatically opens their web browser, causes them to go online (we hope), and submits their answers to a database on my web site.

➤ 4. Use Cookies Strategically

Another information-gathering strategy is to use *cookies*. Cookies are tiny pieces of information that can be placed on your site visitor's web browser for retrieval later. These are widely used to display banners, keep track of shopping carts, remember passwords, track affiliate referrals, and so on. Let's say you want to learn how many of the people who responded to a certain ad actually made a purchase. One way to do this is to create a special web page URL for the ad. When someone clicks on the ad URL, they come to the special page where JavaScript code places a cookie on their web browser indicating that they came from a certain ad. When a purchase is made in the site-ordering system the cookie (if any) is retrieved and a record is made of the source of the sale.

➤ 5. Examine Order Files

Another way to learn about visitor shopping patterns is to analyze individual order files as well as summaries. Once a visitor places an order or provides an e-mail address, any information collected about that individual can be used to develop a personal profile. Amazon.com uses such information to offer recommendations of other books or purchases based on previous purchases.

➤ 6. Provide Site Personalization

Larger company sites are employing database tools that harvest information about visitors by what products they look at or purchase, which banners they click on, and so on. Then this data is merged with other databases providing demographic information by zip code, for example, to give a customer profile. More about the possibilities for data mining can be studied in the book *Data Mining Your Website* by Jesus Mena (Digital Press, 1999).

➤ 7. Study Your Traffic Logs

Considerable data about your customers and their surfing habits can be gained from studying the traffic logs for your web site. These can tell you how the visitor came to your site, browser used, route used to surf through your web site, most popular pages, domain name of visitors, and much more.

➤ 8. Employ JavaScript on Your Site

In addition to placing cookies, JavaScript can be programmed to harvest information contained in the visitor's web browser, such as plug-ins available, the resolution of the computer monitor, operating system used, and version of browser.

The information you learn from each of these methods can help you gain a clearer picture of those visiting your site. Use the data with integrity; adhere to your privacy policy, but use what you learn about your visitors to fine-tune your web site sales and revenues, and you'll come out ahead. Careful attention to customer data is a major factor in distinguishing successful from unsuccessful sites. Neglect it at your peril.

■ Elements of a Customer Profile

Here are some elements of a customer profile to consider. For business-to-consumer businesses these customers are individuals. Of course, business-to-business (B2B) customers are companies, but they usually have a human face that may well have some specific characteristics as owner, purchasing agent, engineer, webmaster, or VP of marketing.

➤ Important Parameters

Let's begin to define your customers with some of these parameters:

Geographic. Are they grouped regionally, nationally, globally?

Cultural and ethnic. What languages do they prefer to do business in? Does ethnicity affect their tastes or buying behaviors?

Economic conditions, income and/or purchasing power. What is the average household income or purchasing power of your customers? What are the economic conditions they face as individuals? As an industry?

Power. What is the decision-making level and title of your typical B2B customer?

Size of company. What company size are you best able to serve? Do you determine this best by annual revenue or number of employees?

Age. What is the age of the companies you do business with? Dot-com start-ups or several decades old? What is the predominant age group of your target buyers? How many children and of what age are in the family?

Values, attitudes, beliefs. What are the predominant values that your customers have in common? What is their attitude toward your kind of product or service?

Knowledge and awareness. How much knowledge do your customers have about your product or service, about your industry? How much education is needed? How much brand-building advertising do you need to make your pool of customers aware of what you offer?

Lifestyle. How many lifestyle characteristics can you name about your purchasers? CACI (www.caci.com) has devel-

oped the fascinating ACORN (www.premierinsights
.com/acorn.html) system of 43 closely targeted lifestyle
profiles that can be tied to specific zip codes. If you were
to geocode your existing customer database using their
ACORN system, you would be able to determine patterns for your best customers that would guide future
marketing.

Buying patterns. There is a growing body of information
on how consumers of different ages and demographic
groups shop on the Web. This is vital information for
your marketing plan, even if you have to pay to get it.
Links to some of that information can be found in our
E-Commerce Research Room (www.wilsonweb.com/
research).

Media used. How do your targeted customers learn? What
do they read? What magazines do they subscribe to?
What are their favorite web sites? These are all pretty
obvious in developing a marketing campaign.

I've just touched the surface here, but I hope it gives you
an idea of the process. So once for good measure, all repeat
together: "The core of our Internet Marketing Plan is understanding our customers." Get this right and you can carve out
a successful business on the Web. Be careless in defining
your customers, and you'll doom your online marketing, no
matter how much money you throw at it.

■ Online Demographic Resources

- American Demographics. (www.marketingtools.com)
- Web marketing demographic studies. Links to hundreds of articles and demographic studies online (www

.wilsonweb.com/cat/cat.cfm?page = 1&subcat = mm_ Demograf)
- Shopper Online Buying Behaviors (subscribers only). Links to hundreds of articles and studies of online shopper behavior. (www.wilsonweb.com/research/)
- CyberAtlas. (www.cyberatlas.com)
- Nua Internet Surveys. (www.nua.ie)

■ Determining Customer Lifetime Value

About a year ago my college-age daughter joined a well-known CD club, attracted by their 12-CDs-for-1-cent offer. She had to agree to purchase a minimum of six CDs at regular price within two years. She's already completed her initial minimum and has spent about $200 with a year to go. I would guess that she's not atypical.

Can you imagine how radical it was the first time a Marketing Director proposed such a huge kind of giveaway to the CEO?

"You're going to give away that much product for free?" shouts the CEO, now on his feet. "That's outrageous! That would cost us at least $25.00 per customer."

"$27.32, actually, sir, including shipping and handling," recites the Marketing Director timidly.

"How do we know they won't just take it and run, and never buy a thing more from us?" blusters the CEO.

"Experience, sir. We've calculated the average Customer Lifetime Value for our existing customers," he replies, trying to keep his cool, "and it's $100 over two years. We'll lose some money the first year, but gain it back as that customer continues to purchase from us. In fact, sir," he continues, feeling more confident as he goes, "this plan will gain us four times as many customers as our former marketing plan, and by the second year begin to increase revenue by 60%." (Note: these figures are merely for sake of example, and do not represent any particular business.)

➤ How to Determine the Customer Lifetime Value

Now don't get me wrong. I'm not suggesting that you suddenly give away products. But I am proposing that you determine the Customer Lifetime Value for your own business as accurately as possible. This is how:

1. Compute your average profit per sale (total sales revenue minus advertising, marketing, and product or service fulfillment expenses, divided by number of sales).

2. Determine how many times the average customer will purchase from you, say, over a two-year period.

3. Calculate the amount of profit you make from that customer in two years.

Actually, the number you come up with will be high, since it includes all the advertising expenses necessary to stimulate sales from new and existing customers, and getting that first purchase is the most expensive. After that your customers are inclined to purchase from you, and once you have an address you can target-market to them much less expensively than to the general public. Your existing customers also generate new customers from their referrals. If there's a way to quantify all this, it gives you valuable information.

However, you can make some estimates. The more accurate the data you input, the more reliable the result. Unfortunately, there's no easy way to accurately predict the Customer Lifetime Value for a start-up. You'll need to start with some educated guesses based on careful research and the experience of others.

➤ **What It Tells You**

Why is this so important? Because if you know that each customer will bring you $38 profit over a two-year period, then you can afford to break even or even lose money on the first sale in order to acquire the customer, since you know that on average you'll make it up later.

Marketing wizard Jay Abraham puts it this way in his book *Getting Everything You Can Out of All You've Got* (St. Martins Press, 2000): "Until you identify and understand exactly how much combined profit a client represents to your business for the life of that relationship, you can't begin to know how much time, effort, and, most importantly, expense you can afford to invest to acquire that client in the first place."

Once you know your Customer Lifetime Value, you'll know how much you can afford to spend—or lose—to get that first sale. And that knowledge is priceless. I'm convinced that this one single fact—the lifetime value of your customer—is absolutely vital to an intelligent marketing campaign. Without this knowledge, you're shooting in the dark; with this knowledge, you'll be willing to take the short-term risks necessary in order to achieve long-term gain.

Exercise: Estimate your own online business's Customer Lifetime Value. The results are sure to help you look at your marketing plan more realistically.

■ Knowing Your Customers

Author Joanne Gucwa, President of Technology Management Associates, Inc., has some tips to help you get a better handle on what your customers are thinking.

How do you get to know your customers? How do you find out what they want? The simple answer: Talk with them. The sophisticated answer: Talk with them.

One secret lies in practicing a variation of the Golden Rule. "Do unto others as you want them to do unto you." That is, communicate with your customers and prospects in the medium they wish to receive and they'll respond. Ask the right questions—frequently—and they will tell you what you need to know. The other secret is leveraging the information you obtain.

➤ Medium

Although technology's siren song may be wonderfully alluring, your customers live in a multimedia, time-pressed, yet human and emotional world. You need to use multiple media to reach your customers and provide multiple options for their return response—and engage them in a continuing dialog with you in the *way* they want and *when* they want. Put out your message via e-mail, telephone, regular mail, fax, or web site, and allow your customers to respond in any way they choose—not necessarily with the same medium you used to reach them. For example, you may pose a question on your web site, but many engaged customers want to pick up the phone and call an 800 number.

➤ The Right Questions

After 27 years of asking questions in the industrial marketplace, I've discovered *one* question that elicits more good customer feedback than any other: "If there were one thing about our product or service (or whatever) you could change, what would that be?"

Far more powerful than "how can we improve?" or "what would you like to see in the next upgrade?," this simple, open-ended question lets you know (a) what the dissatisfiers are in your offering, (b) what will keep this particular customer coming back for more, and (c) what threats your competitors could pose should they offer this change.

➤ Leverage

Everyone talks about the rapid change the Internet is undergoing. The Internet is also causing your customers to change along with it. Expectations rise with each new announced improvement. Thus the research you conducted last week may no longer be valid, and your customer may have moved beyond what you were told a few weeks ago. What to do?

You don't need an expensive knowledge management system, or even a fancy customized database. What you *do* need is a process for: (1) identifying your best customers—those 20% who provide you 80% of your profit; and (2) making sure you contact those best customers whenever an important event happens in your industry—or at least once a quarter—and immediately updating their feedback in a centralized location, even if it's no more than a contact management program such as ACT! posted on your secure intranet.

Joanne Gucwa is president of Technology Management Associates, Inc. (www.techmanage.com) of Chicago. TMA provides business information and technology tracking services. She may be reached at jogucwa @techmanage.com or (312) 984-5050.

Exercise: After you've collected this kind of information from a wide variety of sources, write a description of the specific characteristics that differentiate the best 20% of your customers from the others. Distill all you've learned into a maximum of three or four paragraphs, even though you may have spent days or weeks researching. Then list three ways you can contact those people or businesses.

Part III

Market and Product Focus

You've studied your customers' characteristics. Now you need to design your products (goods and services) to meet their perceived needs precisely. In this section you'll learn to segment the market into particular customer needs and then clearly differentiate your products from one another and from your competitors' products.

Chapter

Segmenting Your Internet Market

Once you've studied the customers who are likely to purchase your products or services, you may find that there are several kinds of customers, each with different interests and needs. It pays you big rewards to be aware of these differences and adjust your marketing strategies accordingly. When you segment your market in this way, you increase your chances of success.

■ Segmenting Golf Shoppers

Let's say you own a golf store on the Internet. You can assume that your customers play golf, but that probably isn't enough. Golfers have many differences, and their purchasing habits have a lot to do with these differences. I was intrigued by the questions asked by Wilson Sporting Goods in a marketing survey (no longer available) where you could receive free golf balls just for answering a few simple questions. The Wilson Sporting Goods people asked:

Age

Gender

Handicap level

Whether you play on public or private golf courses

Number of rounds of golf per year

Manufacturer of your current irons

Shaft type

Current choice of golf balls

Of course, Wilson Sporting Goods is doing market research from a manufacturer's, not a retailer's, standpoint. But you could learn a lot from the results of this survey (which I'm not privy to). You'd probably find various groupings based on age and gender. Young golfers probably make different kinds of purchases and for different reasons than older golfers. Female golfers have different needs than male golfers. The handicap level will tell you how good the players are. Public or private courses (and perhaps brand of irons) tell you income level. Rounds per year tells you how serious they are about the game.

Let's say you were to do this kind of survey in your online golf store and found that these were your primary customer groups (this is entirely fictional, intended as an example only):

Wealthy males, aged 60 to 75, who play an average of 70 times per year	34%
Moderate income males, aged 35 to 50, who play about 24 times per year	27%
Moderate income females, aged 60 to 75, who play an average of 45 times per year	22%
Other	17%

What does this tell you about what products you need to carry in your store? Where you need to advertise? How you need to divide up your store browsing sections?

■ Segmenting Newsletter Subscribers

I learned more about market segmentation when I discovered that there were several types of potential subscribers to my paid *Web Commerce Today* newsletter subscription.

Newbies needing a quick e-commerce education	48%
Consultants and those with company e-commerce responsibility	15%
Current online storeowners and developers seeking to improve an existing store	13%
Those preparing an e-commerce business plan	13%
Other	11%

For about two years my marketing plan had been designed generically, to sell to anyone who might be interested in purchasing my newsletter subscription and obtaining access to my E-Commerce Research Room. When I began to market to each of these groups separately, my subscription rate increased about 70%. (Take a look at www.wilsonweb .com/wct to see the different sales tracks for each segment.)

■ Segmenting Types of Site Visitors

From a Web marketing standpoint, one of the difficulties you face when you offer a number of products aimed at different groups is segmenting visitors quickly and moving them into their own section. Imagine the problems with a company as diverse as Microsoft (www.microsoft.com), for example (see Figure 12.1). Their web site uses these kinds of categories:

Product Family Sites	Customer Sites	Web Services
Windows	Home & Personal	Office eServices
Office	Business	Windows Update
Servers	IT Professional Developer	bCentral
Developer Tool	Partner/Reseller Education	MSN

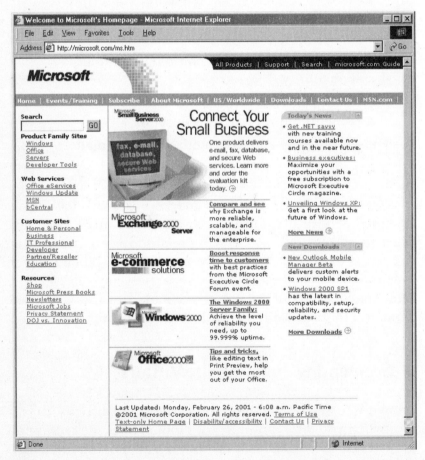

Figure 12.1 Microsoft.com (Screen shot reprinted by permission from Microsoft Corporation.)

Notice the redundant way they segment by both product/ service family and customer type. I think Microsoft does a pretty good job at this.

When you go to IBM (www.ibm.com), you find this breakdown (see Figure 12.2):

Resources For:

Home/home office

Small business

Large business

Government

Developers

IBM business partners

Jobs at IBM

Figure 12.2   IBM.com (Reproduced by permission from IBM.com. Copyright © 2001 by International Business Machines Corporation.)

Investors

Journalists

You can see that IBM has four classes of customers: enterprise, government, home/home office, and small business, and markets to each of them differently. Within each category will be the products particularly designed for that particular class of customers.

■ Product Segmentation

One of the best examples of product segmentation is Reebok shoes (www.reebok.com). When you go to the web site it provides 13 different categories: basketball, adventure, baseball, fitness, golf, running, soccer, tennis, walking, football, classic, track and field, and kids. Within each of these categories is a whole series of products tailored to customers with a particular sports focus. The better the customers see your products meeting their specific needs, the easier it will be for them to make a purchase.

One of the most profitable exercises you can conduct is to segment your site visitors into specific categories. This takes market research on your customers and then careful analysis, but it will enable you to be much more successful in your web site marketing efforts. Then include in your Internet Marketing Plan a paragraph or two explaining how you segment your potential customers. Later in the Plan you'll indicate which products or services are most suitable for each segment, and a marketing strategy to reach each segment of your market.

Exercise: List three to six segments of your particular market; then create a sentence explaining why you chose these particular segments.

Chapter

Differentiating Your Company's Products and Services

To succeed online, you need to make your company and its products distinct from similar Internet businesses. Here are some tips on achieving that differentiation.

"The greatest single factor in a new product's failure is the lack of significant 'points of difference' that set it apart from competitors' substitutes," say Eric Berkowitz and fellow authors, in their best-selling textbook *Marketing* (Irwin, 1997). This applies not only to products and services, but to a web site. How are casual web surfers going to perceive your online business as distinct from a thousand others they might click on in their online shopping excursions?

Another way to approach differentiation is in terms of *branding*, an advertising industry buzzword that means much the same thing. But for now we'll go with "differentiating your company's products and services."

■ Your USP

Developing a clear Unique Selling Proposition has a lot to do with differentiating your web site from others. I look at some of the major players in the online marketing information field where I compete, and I see some clear attempts at differentiation.

■ Logo

ClickZ Network (www.clickz.com). Distinctive Z with an arrow alongside.

eMarketer (www.emarketer.com). Distinctive red ball with "e" on it, with consistent red, white, and black color scheme.

Channel Seven (www.channelseven.com). Distinctive logotype font with site name.

Iconocast (www.iconocast.com). Distinctive logo of Atlas bearing a microwave antenna.

JimWorld.com (www.jimworld.com). No single logo.

Wilson Internet Services (www.wilsonweb.com). Small logotype plus photo of author.

■ Statement

ClickZ. "The ultimate resource for doing business online."

eMarketer. "Where business begins online."

Channel Seven. "The information source for Internet marketing and advertising decision makers."

Iconocast. "eMarketing intelligence for intelligent marketers."

JimWorld. No clear overarching statement.

WilsonWeb. "We provide key information about doing business on the Net—hundreds of articles, thousands of links to resources on e-commerce and Web marketing."

■ Distinctives

ClickZ. Focus on Internet advertising and marketing professionals. Regular columnists with a variety of points of view. Daily e-mail.

eMarketer. Provides a variety of services for marketers, including news headlines, statistics, community, articles, and paid reports. Weekly e-mail, with daily stats and news.

Channel Seven. Serves professionals in the online advertising industry. News, articles, analysis of ad campaigns. Daily e-mail.

Iconocast. "The definitive source for facts, figures, trend analysis, and insider information in the Internet marketing industry." Concise profiles of various industries, plus insider gossip. Weekly e-mail.

JimWorld. Helpful collection of resources, especially focused on the needs of webmasters and small business site owners. Semi-monthly e-mail.

WilsonWeb. Collection of articles, an articles database, and three newsletters with an educative "how-to" approach to Web marketing, e-commerce, and e-business. Primary focus on small to medium businesses. Semi-monthly and weekly e-mail.

Besides these, there are thousands of other marketing information sites. The best have their own distinctive flavors, looks, and feels. Some have excellent weekly or monthly newsletters, often with a distinct focus. But many sites look like a thousand others, and tend to all blur together. I make it a point to visit many of these sites each month, and they blur together for me, too!

■ A Memorable Name

To stand out from others, businesses and products need distinctive, memorable names. If the name isn't memorable, it's hard to differentiate yourself. See more about this in the chapter on "Naming Your Online Business."

■ Distinctive Packaging

Many small businesspeople cut corners on web site design costs. The result is a same old, lookalike web site that you can't remember an hour after you visited it. Like cereal boxes that vie for consumers' attention, web sites need strong visual images. Several of the marketing information sites listed above feature professionally designed logos that provide instant recognition. A small businessperson can get a logo designed for $200 to $500, though many companies spend several thousand dollars on the process, since it is so vital to the distinctiveness of their companies and their products. Most graphic design companies offer this service.

Just as important as a logo is a distinctive design for the web site. The site ought to leave you with an attractive visual memory. Take a look at several distinctive sites that achieve this; then look at your own. See Dan Janal's site (www .janal.com), for example (see Figure 13.1).

Sometimes computer professionals double as designers. You need to realize that learning Photoshop is technology; design is art. You want the artist to learn the technology, rather than trying to teach the techie artistic taste and flair. Insist on a graphic designer who already has web graphics experience. Of course, the graphics need to be modest in file size and serve your marketing purpose, but they need to create an attractive look and feel, a distinctive ambience, a memory that lingers.

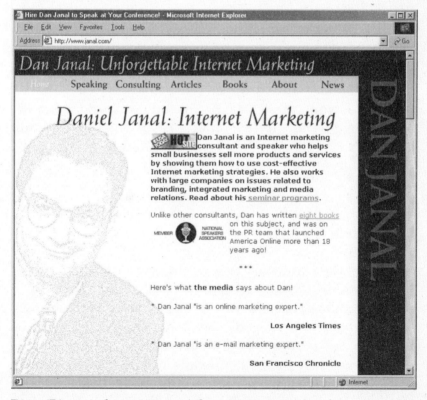

Figure 13.1   Janal.com (Copyright © 2001, Dan Janal Communications. All rights reserved.)

■ A Distinct Voice

Another way to differentiate your web site is with a distinctive "voice." What I mean by voice is interjecting personality and individuality in the web site text. Now in many corporate cultures this is taboo. "We must use corporate-speak. No individual is important, it's the *company*." The problem is that the *company* isn't very interesting by itself. So companies that are smart find spokespersons who pitch their products, i.e., distinctive "voices," such as Kmart, Martha Stewart, Sprint, and Michael Jordan.

They aren't trading just on the star's popularity, but the star's personality and likability. Companies even invent a distinctive voice with their logo or mascot: Kentucky Fried Chicken (The Colonel), Jack in the Box ("Jack," Styrofoam head and all), Wendy's (Dave), and Taco Bell (talking Mexican chihuahua—since dropped like a hot pepper).

What is your site's "voice"? You might consider finding professional writers to help craft a clearly delineated point of view. Perhaps ghostwrite for the CEO or someone else who can give the site personality and distinctiveness.

■ A Clear Focus

Part of making your business or product distinctive is narrowing. Some online businesses try to be everything to everyone and fail because they just can't succeed in differentiating themselves as generalists. Actually, the larger the company, the harder it is to be distinctive. Marketers for a smaller, narrowly focused company have a much easier job than those saddled with a lumbering giant. That's why we see a trend toward breaking up larger companies into smaller business units.

Look at your own online offering. Let's say that in the real world you sell all kinds of insurance. That's because what *local* businesses need is a generalist. But online if you bill yourself as selling general insurance products you've just digitally signed your company's online death warrant. Online you need to specialize in selling insurance for bungee jumpers or insurance for less-than-10-day trips to Mexico. Make it clear. Make it specific. Concentrate on a narrow area and you can become distinctive and able to differentiate yourself from all the other companies out there. There's nothing that says you can't start different web sites to market different products. Just make each web site's focus clear and concentrated.

Exercise: Write down the 10 leading online businesses that are similar to yours. Then characterize the distinctiveness of each. Now look for ways to make your online business stand out from all the rest. Outline the steps you can take within three months to make your site and online products or services distinctive.

■ Recommended Reading: Differentiate or Die

Differentiate or Die: Survival in Our Era of Killer Competition (Jack Trout with Steve Rivkin, John Wiley & Sons, Inc., 2000, hardcover, 230 pages)

I have long contended that successful web sites will clearly distinguish themselves from others with a concisely stated Unique Selling Proposition (USP). So I was particularly happy to read Jack Trout's *Differentiate or Die.* If you've read Ries and Trout's *22 Immutable Laws of Marketing* and *Positioning: The Battle for Your Mind,* you've seen some of this before. Trout's strengths can be called branding, positioning, or differentiation—they're all closely related. In this book he integrates learnings from both offline and online businesses.

Trout and his coauthor Steve Rivkin contend that the only way a company can survive is to differentiate. This is true even more on the Internet where a business's competitors are not limited by driving distance but encompass all the similar web sites in the site owner's country—and, to a smaller degree, all the similar web sites in the world. First the authors discuss the USP, with the focus on a USP for a specific advertisement. Too many creative ads, they say, don't clearly state a product's unique selling points.

The next several chapters look at various approaches to differentiating a product or company. Trout and Rivkin explain why quality, customer orientation, and creativity aren't usually effective. Price may be the initial approach that differentiates a product, but most companies that begin with low prices eventually move to more moderate pricing after establishing themselves. Differentiating with a higher price, ironically, is more successful. Breadth of product line is not an effective way for most companies to differentiate.

Next the authors explain the four steps to differentiate: (1) make sense in the context of the market as it exists, (2) find the differentiating idea, (3) be able to support and demonstrate the differentiating idea, and (4) communicate your difference.

Trout and Rivkin then list differentiating ideas that *do* work effectively, and give a number of helpful examples of each: (1) being first or number one, (2) owning a particular attribute or product quality in the consumer's mind, (3) demonstrating product leadership, (4) drawing upon an impressive company history or heritage, (5) focusing on a particular market specialty, (6) showing that your product is the preference of influential persons or groups, (7) focusing on a product's unique ingredients, (8) being the new generation of products, or (9) being popular or hot.

Finally, the authors demonstrate how company growth can destroy its differences unless company leaders are careful. They note that differentiation requires sacrifice; future directions in marketing must not blur the difference. Also, how a product is differentiated or branded in one country may need to be substantially different to succeed in another culture.

For online companies struggling to obtain a unique and clear identity in the sea of similar dot-coms, the book *Differentiate or Die* is timely. Reading and taking heed may well save your company from death, and hopefully push it forward into sharp definition in the public's mind. Strongly recommended.

Chapter 14

Naming Your Online Business

Somewhere in the process of finding a suitable online niche for your business, studying your competitors, and determining ways to differentiate your online business, it comes time to name the fledgling business.

Don't get this backwards. I've met a few business-fools who own some nifty domain names and want to start a business to fit the names. Wrong. Without a niche and a sound business idea, you don't have a chance of success—even with a good domain name. You're much better off to sell unneeded domain names to someone who can use them (or someone foolish enough to hold them for ransom).

■ Step 1. Develop a Clear, Simple Statement Describing Your Business

See Chapter 6, "Developing a Unique Sales Proposition." Your USP is basic. Whatever you call it, a positioning statement or

USP will help you name your company. Remember, you don't start with the name, you start with the concept, and the name flows from that.

■ Step 2. List All the Words That Relate to Your Business Idea

Next, list all the words that relate to your business idea, its category, products, services, core audiences, and key differentiating factors. The longer this list, the better you are at loosening up your brain so you can come up with a business name that is striking and memorable.

■ Step 3. Brainstorm Business Name Word Combinations

I don't suggest that you include .com as part of your business name. But since you are creating an e-business, you want your business name to be similar to your domain name.

The chances are that the domain name for each of these keywords has already been taken—by themselves. But now you take the list of words from Step 2 and begin to form two-word combinations. Ideally, you'll come up with a business name that propels you to stand out from the crowd. For many e-businesses, the domain name *is* the company name, though these days it is considered a liability to include the ".com" as part of your corporate name. Let's examine the characteristics of a good domain name.

A good domain name is short. Of course, short is harder and harder to find these days. Short—if you can get it—is important for several reasons. It's easy to fit into logos, makes a better brand, is more easily recognizable, and is harder to misspell. Long is not better, unless you also want to get a domain that spells out your company name in its entirety.

A good domain name is memorable. You remember generic names, such as Art.com and Drugstore.com. But you also remember more unique names such as Amazon.com, Google .com, and FogDog.com. Putting together strange combinations of words is fun and can be very productive. It helps if it rhymes like FogDog, or repeats sounds such as Google, or is singsongy like WilsonWeb. Say your prospective domain name out loud to listen to its sounds. You also need to find if your tongue gets twisted around any syllables. One of my struggles is with PlanetPayment.com, the service that enables merchants all over the world to take credit cards. I can never remember if payment comes first or planet. And try saying PlanetPayment five times fast. Whatever your domain name, it should stick in the mind.

A good domain name isn't easily confused with others. In our desperation to find a domain name we accept hyphenated names, .net substitutes, and put "the" in front of a word, as in TheStandard.com. The problem is confusion. Trademark laws are designed to prevent customer confusion. If the holder of a similar domain name is first to trademark his combination, it could threaten your domain name, or at least your ability to use it as a brand. Another consideration is how you'll need to say your domain name over the phone. If you always have to say "spelled ding-hyphen-doodle-dot-com," you'll soon wish you'd left out the hyphens. Do your best to find a name that can't be confused.

A good domain name is hard to misspell. If people can misspell something, they will. The longer and more complex your domain name, the harder it is for your customers to type it in correctly. Many of them can't type well to start with, so to type in a long name may lose you lots of business.

It pays to purchase the misspellings of a domain name, too. Poachers can be driven off by lawsuits if you have trademark protection, but you don't want that expense.

A good domain name relates to your business name or core business. This one's pretty obvious. It's best if your domain name can be guessed from your company name. But in your search for a domain name, don't give up if you can't find the domain for your exact business name. Find functional names, names that describe your uniqueness, names that express an emotion or attitude. The media agency Beyond Interactive couldn't get beyond.com, and beyondinteractive .com is too long (though it points to their site). But they have GoBeyond.com which expresses their company attitude about serving their clients.

A good domain name sounds solid to your target audience. With so many domain names taken, there is a growing market for .cc, .ws, .tv, and .to domain names. (These are the country domains of the small nations of Cocos [Keeling] Islands, [Western] Samoa, Tuvalu, and Tonga, respectively.) The problem is that the general public, in the United States anyway, is accustomed to .com, or maybe .net (though .net and .org aren't nearly as well regarded). Offbeat domain names sound . . . well, offbeat and suspect. When and if the new raft of domain names such as .shop and .web finally appear, they'll come with a good deal of publicity that will cause their gradual acceptance, unlike .cc or .ws. If you have a business in France, of course, you would probably eschew a .com domain and seek one that proudly bears the .fr extension. What sounds solid and established is relative to where you do business.

➤ Getting the Creative Process Going

NameBoy.com is the most fun, creative tool I've come across. You enter a primary and a secondary word to work with, select the type of site you have, and whether or not you want to turn on the rhyming feature—then let 'er rip! It works like one of those children's books that allows you to play with multiple head, body, and leg combinations. NameBoy displays various name combinations in three columns: available names, taken names, and for-sale names. You'll laugh at some of the possible permutations. I inserted "biz" as a primary word and "small" as the secondary word, and came up with seven pages of combinations, including "bizsmall.com," "biz-fizz.com," and "ms-biz.com" (that one won't last). The longest list by far was names for sale, held by domain name speculators with dollar signs in their eyes, the first of which was "biz.com." These crazy searches are free. NameBoy makes its money when you click on your best picks and register them, and perhaps when you purchase them from a broker or at auction. Have fun with this.

Network Solutions' NameFetcher uses synonyms to help you generate new domain ideas, much as a thesaurus would. I put in the three words "small," "business," and "marketing." Then for each word it asked me to give the closest synonym. For "small" I had to select from "brief," "compact," "concise," "delicate," etc. Once I had narrowed down the meaning for each word, NameFetcher fetched the available domain names in .com, .net, and .org varieties. (www.networksolutions.com/purchasing/nameGen.jhtml).

E-gineer Domainator allows you to put together several words of your own choosing (www.e-gineer.com/domainator). Then it searches a series of databases and finds available domains with combinations of these words, domains that have been taken already, including the various hyphenated combinations in .com, .net, .org, and .cc. Next it checks the U.S. Patent and Trademark Office database for any trademarks where all your words are used together. It searches Dictionary.com for a thorough definition, with hyperlinked synonyms for each definition. Next it translates your words into a dozen or so foreign languages, shows various combinations of the words, and finally lists rhymes for each of the words. All this is displayed on one page you could print out. Wow! If you're researching various word combinations for a business name, Domainator can stimulate your thinking in lots of directions. The service is free. They make their money if you use their domain name registration services.

Hopefully, you'll find some word combinations that fit many or most of these criteria. Run them past some other people to see how they react.

➤ Domain Names Are a Marketing Bargain

I consider a good domain name a marketing bargain. ArtUFrame.com bought Art.com and immediately doubled their sales. A memorable, catchy domain name can make a lot of difference in setting you apart from the crowd. When domain names used to cost $70 for two years (and at Network Solutions, they still do), the cost was a barrier to the smallest businesses. But with domain name registration for now at $10 to $15 per year, securing a domain name—or several you might need—is a bargain that just may not come by again.

➤ Good Names, Bad Names

I'm a bit mystified at companies that name their products or business with words that don't have any meaning in their target language. At the risk of offending, let's look at Hewlett Packard's new company, Agilent Technologies (http://www .agilent.com).

I'm guessing that Agilent is a combination of the word "agile" and a common English suffix. It expresses HP's corporate desire to move quickly and agilely to innovate in the Internet space. But "agile" isn't immediately obvious unless you think about it. Nor does it express a clear category, product, or service. To be fair, HP needed a name that bridged more than one category. But in order to firmly imprint and position "Agilent" in their potential customer's mind, they're going to have to rely entirely on spending hard advertising dollars to make the name familiar, since they're starting nearly from scratch. Small businesses have the advantage: Their names can help position them and be memorable.

➤ Domain Names as Branding

Small business domain thinkers often forget that their domain name automatically becomes their brand name, whether they intend it or not. It will forever after affect how your company is perceived. The time you take to select your name is time well spent. The money you spend for marketing or branding consultants to help you get the very best name is a good investment, too.

Your brand shouldn't sound stodgy. Reading music isn't enough. A good name should be able to sing. Let me illustrate.

Wilson Internet Services. When I named my business Wilson Internet Services in mid-1995, I can't say I found a distinctive name. It sounds pretty generic, and I'm sometimes confused with an Internet Service Provider. When I look back on it, I think that kind of naming was a mistake. I named the company without a clue that I was naming a brand.

People often use my domain name, Wilsonweb.com, rather than my company name. The domain name was a happy confluence of several factors, a kind of singsong, rhythmic, memorable name that has served me well. But I've made mistakes since then, too.

Web Marketing Today. My next attempt was *Web Marketing*

Today® (wilsonweb.com/wmt/), my flagship e-mail market-ing newsletter. It's better. Each word in the name adds to the meaning. And it's somewhat memorable. The domain name webmarketingtoday.com is pretty clumsy, but the publica-tion name has served me very well and is widely known.

Web Commerce Today. When I named my premier e-commerce newsletter *Web Commerce Today*® (wilsonweb .com/wct) in 1997, I made another kind of branding mis-take. The publication has been a tremendous success, but the name hasn't helped at all. I wanted to build on my success and reputation with Web Marketing Today, but I succeeded in confusing people. The name didn't provide a clear way to distinguish between my two publications.

Some time ago I was talking with my friend Ken Evoy, author of the best-selling *Make Your Site Sell* (http:// sales.sitesell.com/myss). He told me, "Even though I've read your newsletters carefully for years, I still don't really know what's the difference between *Web Marketing Today* and *Web Commerce Today*." I was stunned. Why not? It's clear to me what the difference is! It's all about e-commerce! But it wasn't clear to Ken or thousands of others.

I had tried to create a "family" name that related *Web Commerce Today* to my flagship publication. But it wasn't dif-ferent enough. Once I realized this, I worked to differentiate the two more clearly. The more clearly I am able to differen-tiate *Web Commerce Today* from its sister publication, the easier it is to sell. Naming has a lot to do with product differ-entiation.

By 2000, however, I was beginning to understand the importance of branding. I launched two publications, the weekly *JesusWalk: Disciple Lessons from Luke's Gospel* and *DoctorEbiz,* a weekly Q&A column for small business about doing business online. In each case I looked for word combi-nations that would explain exactly what the product was about, and I feel I succeeded pretty well:

Jesus Walk®. The words indicated the goal, to help individuals learn about Jesus from simulating the kind of training that his twelve disciples internalized by just walking along with him. The name is memorable, descriptive, and simple (www.jesuswalk.com).

Doctor Ebiz® played off several factors. First, my own identity as possessing a doctorate. Second, it broadened my focus beyond both Web marketing and e-commerce to e-business, the direction I see things going in the future. The words indicate that this is an e-business doctor, someone who helps diagnose and cure e-business problems. And that's exactly what this weekly column is designed to do.

My family liked the name "Doc Ebiz," but when I asked my friend Michel Fortin, "The Success Doctor" (www.successdoctor.com), he observed that "Doctor Ebiz" has a kind of mnemonic, easy-to-remember quality. It also has a kind of verbal rhythm that can survive being said ten times in rapid succession without turning into mush.

The name is memorable, descriptive, and simple. The only problem with the name is that "doctor" can be abbreviated and the name can be hyphenated in different ways, which required me to secure a number of domain names for the most common misspellings.

To differentiate *Doctor Ebiz* from my other publications, I gave it a different format. It is a question-and-answer piece, short, and with a purposeful maximum of 700 words of content—a quick read, substantially shorter than my other e-zines. It's focused squarely on small business owners who want to succeed online, a huge and growing market.

Remember, your online business name may be different from the name of your traditional business. You may need to file with your local government for a Fictitious Business Name Statement for a new business name, and list your old business name "D.B.A." (doing business as) the online company name—but that's usually not too expensive. Don't be blocked by a poor existing business name; take advantage of going online to brand your business well.

■ Step 4. Check Domain Name Availability

Only when you have developed a number of possible company (or product) names should you begin the domain name search. The reason is this: So many good domain names are taken already, that you may be influenced to only use what is left over. A good place to check your domain name possibilities is the Whois database at www.000domains.com. I used to routinely use the Whois database at Network Solutions, but found that they no longer list full domain ownership information about domain names not registered with them. For other than .com, .net, and .org domain names, consult a domain name registrar in your country (www.norid.no/domreg.html).

Check all of your top name choices, and minor variations of them. Note which domain names are available as a .com (or with your country designation, such as .fr or .de). Also note which have already been purchased. These days there are many more domain names than there are active web sites. In most cases, overeager domain speculators have bought up blocks of names, and are having a difficult time unloading them at the level of prices they were hoping for.

■ Step 5. Check Trademark Availability

In conjunction with deciding on a business name and a corresponding domain name, make sure you check the trademark database for your country. You can also find databases online for most countries. Make sure you cover your own country first, then other countries where you want to avoid confusion. Some online databases are:

US Patent and Trademark Office (http://tess.uspto.gov/bin/gate.exe?f=tess&state=6a1nm0.1.1)

Canada (http://strategis.ic.gc.ca/cgi-bin/sc_consu/trademarks/search_e.pl)

UK (www.patent.gov.uk/dbservices/tm.html)

Australia (www.ipaustralia.gov.au/trademarks/T_srch.htm)

More international links from Gregory H. Guillot, Chartered (www.ggmark.com)

■ Step 6. Purchase Relevant Domain Name(s)

I used to be concerned about the price of a domain name getting jacked up if I were to show an interest. No more. This is how I suggest you handle it. Find out the owner from the Whois directory and then write an e-mail kind of like this:

Dear domain owner,

I've been thinking about starting an online business selling sheetrock screws to contractors. I've come up with about a dozen really good possible domain names, one of which is yours. If you're interested in selling, I'd like to see if we can come to an agreement about price. Fortunately, since I've identified a dozen good domain names, I'm not under pressure to purchase the one you own, but if your price is right, it might help me select yours, and put some fast cash in your pocket.

Sincerely,
John Uptight
Sheet rock screws par excellence!

This way you don't sound too eager, but willing to deal, and the domain name owner knows you have other options, so he can't push the price up too high. I think domain name speculative prices are nosediving as fast as the NASDAQ stock exchange—except for the very best names. Venture capital funding initially drove up prices and created greed in the speculators. But VC money has pretty well dried up for start-ups, and there are many, many domain names waiting for a business. My guess is that if you were to get your hoped-for domain name appraised by Domain Appraisal System (www.solutionhome.com/appraisal) for about $15, you could use that as leverage to purchase a pretty good name for your business. You also should consider having others appraise your domain name picks at Afternic.com (www .afternic.com). Purchasing the domain name may cost you $100 or $250 or $500 or $1,000 depending upon the owner's and your respective negotiating abilities, but a memorable domain name is an important marketing investment—don't skimp here!

■ Step 7. Apply for a Trademark

A trademark is a graphic logo or a unique name that is used in trade to identify a business, product, or service. In general, the first company to use a name in trade owns it. If you plan to use a trademark, you should place the letters "TM" in superscript next to the trade name to indicate your intention to use it as a trademark. The letters "SM" indicate "service mark," though the usage often blurs with that of the word "trademark." To protect your right to use a particular business name, you ought to register the trademark with the official government agency in your country and other countries where you expect to do much business. In the United

States this could cost $300 to $750 or more (including search and attorney fees) and can take a year or two to be completed. If you are successful, and your trademark is registered, you are entitled to use the ® symbol to indicate registration of your trademark.

Many online businesses have learned the hard way that it's cheaper to register the trademark up-front than to wait until another company files for registration ahead of you. If you can't afford the filing and legal costs, I understand, but make this one of your early priorities as soon as some revenue is generated, if it looks like your business has commercial potential.

Just because you own a domain name doesn't automatically mean you own the corresponding trademark. Since your business, by definition, will be national or international when you get on the Internet, you can't afford to ignore the legal threats you may face to your unique business name. More information is available at www.wilsonweb .com/cat/cat.cfm?page = 1&subcat = mm_Law. If you're interested in U.S. trademark law, you might read the book *Trademark: Legal Care for Your Business and Product Name* (Nolo Press, 1999), by Kate McGrath and Stephen Elias, or these authors' *Trademark Registration Kit* (Quick & Legal Series, Nolo Press, 1999).

I hope this will help you see the process involved in naming your online business. As one who has made some serious marketing mistakes here, I hope that my advice will save you some headaches. Remember, the main costs of naming your business are:

Fictitious business name statement. Local government. $10 to $50.

Domain name. $10 to $500 or more, depending upon your country, and the price you have to pay for an already owned domain name.

Trademark registration. $300 to $750 or more, depending upon your country, and whether you file forms yourself or get legal assistance.

Make sure you don't scrimp where it counts.

Exercise: If you haven't named your business yet, go through the steps outlined in this chapter to arrive at two or three possible names.

Chapter 15

Building Trust in an Unknown Web Business

Trust is the single indispensable element of doing business. You've got to generate trust in order to build your business online. Fortunately there are ways to do this effectively.

National and international brands take millions of dollars to be recognized, and billions to become household names. Expensive? Yes. But these brands now transmit instant trust that make shoppers willing, even eager, to buy.

Is there any way small businesses can match the power of these megabrands? No, not really. Small businesses will get a narrow slice of the pie, but even that narrow slice of a national or international market can be plenty to sustain the business and cause it to flourish.

The key to competing is to build trust with your site visitor from the time he or she happens upon your web site until the decision to buy is made—and even afterward through the fulfillment of the product ordered.

To succeed in building trust, you must plan and execute a deliberate Web marketing strategy. It doesn't have to be expensive to be very effective. These are the elements of the strategy: a site that builds trust, a personal feel that builds trust, an ordering policy that builds trust, and associations that build trust.

■ Designing a Site That Builds Trust

If trust is the lubrication that is necessary for business to take place, then you can do a lot to build that trust by the way you design and lay out your online store.

➤ Have a Professional Design Your Online Store

When you're looking for a store to shop in, a lot of little things catch your eye. Even clues so subtle that they don't reach the conscious level contribute to the impression you form. The sign, the way the windows are placed, the parking lot, the general look of neatness or clutter, the colors, the window display. You're attracted to stores that radiate a feeling of competency and success. You shun stores that look tumbledown, temporary, tasteless, and tacky.

Online stores are judged by their layout and design. They can look amateurish or professional. An amateurish look raises all sorts of questions in your customers' minds about whether they will receive any product at all, and whether they will receive satisfaction if the product isn't what they expected. An attractive web site design, on the other hand, exudes a sense of competence and inspires confidence in your customer.

Professional web site design for an online store may not be as expensive as you think. Many online stores these days are built in template format, so the design for a single page, once set, carries through the entire store. To find a professional web site designer, look in your local Yellow Pages under "Internet" or "Web Site Services," or in your city's local section of the Yahoo! directory under Business and Shopping | Business to Business | Communications and Networking.

➤ Sell Brand Name Products

Another way to generate trust is to carry name brand products. People buy brands they have confidence in, and that confidence rubs off on the store that carries those brands. Cheap knockoffs and off-brands will raise questions about the quality of your business.

Of course, a company that is selling a new product or carries products by an unknown manufacturer is at a disadvantage. Expensive branding efforts *do* affect customer perception of the store that carries those goods. You'll need to demonstrate that products by unknown manufacturers are equal or superior to the established brands. The burden is on the store owner to make the case. Brands breed confidence.

➤ Make Credible Presentations

Most customers distrust products promoted with hype and unbelievable claims. Though exaggeration can be effective with some shoppers, with many, wild claims will backfire. The store owner needs to present products in such a way that all of a shopper's anticipated questions are answered in a believable manner.

➤ Provide Full Contact Information

Finally, your design should make it easy to find full contact information—address, phone, e-mail address, and so on. Too many sites restrict ways in which potential customers can ask questions and make contact. This breeds frustration and distrust. Consumers are wary of online stores that hide phone numbers or mailing addresses. The shopper wonders, "If I can't get in touch with this store owner when I have a question, what happens when I have a problem after the sale? Why *aren't* phone calls accepted?" I, too, am wary of companies I can't contact through traditional communications channels.

In order to establish the trust required to make the sale, harness all the tools at your disposal—design, products, presentation, and contact information.

■ A Personal Feel That Builds Trust

Large companies spend tens of millions of dollars to build a brand. This expenditure buys name recognition and the confidence that goes with it, a favorable position or association in the mind of the consumer, and a belief that a company with so much invested in its reputation will not disappoint its customers. Investments in brand development pay rich dividends.

But smaller companies just can't afford the money it takes to establish a national brand. Instead of relying upon an established reputation, they are required to build trust and confidence from the moment a customer lands on their site. Big companies have their brand, but small companies have the advantage of a personal face and personal character to the business; connecting personally can be a very powerful sales motivator indeed!

➤ Show Photos of Yourself or Your Staff

For years I've displayed a photo of myself on my web site. I went to a professional photographer to get as good a photo as

I could. But, frankly, I'm not handsome enough to win customers. I don't display the photo out of vanity. I show it for one reason: so people will perceive me as a person, and therefore begin to establish a relationship with me through my writings.

In a sense, you are what makes your small business different from all the rest. You are your own brand.

You might not want to show a photo of yourself, but perhaps a group photo of your staff or sales team. Professional photos taken for this purpose can project the personal service you give your customers. They put faces behind the name. And people connect with people. Give individuals the choice of doing business with a cheerful, competent person rather than a faceless corporation and they'll choose the person every time.

Even large companies realize this. Wells Fargo talks about "your personal banker," Wal-Mart features its own employees in national TV ads, and Micro Warehouse catalog "brand" includes a picture of one of its phone order-takers (though they've removed that photo from their web site).

If you have an existing brick-and-mortar business, show a photo of the building, too. Even if it doesn't look spectacular, it demonstrates that your business isn't just a cyber-vapor pretending to be an online store.

➤ Show Photos of Happy People on the Front Page

Don't stop with photos of yourself and your staff. Instead of animated letters and blue buttons, provide centers of human interest on your front page. Find photos of happy people who are part of the demographic target group you've determined are your best customers. To see how this is done, take a look at Walmart.com (www.walmart.com; see Figure 15.1). You can secure royalty-free people shots for your web site

Figure 15.1   Walmart.com shows happy people. (Copyright © 2001 Walmart.com, Inc. All rights reserved.)

from PhotoDisc (www.photodisc.com) for about $30 each—a small price to pay for attractive models and excellent photography.

Shoppers will relate to the people they see at your site. If they look confident and at ease, it will help to lessen a shopper's natural distrust of unknown Internet shops.

➤ Tell the Story of Your Business

To build trust you'll also want to tell the story of your business. You may think that shoppers won't care about the details. But it's precisely these details that show your store is for real, that values of honesty and hard work underlie your whole business. I've read some business stories that really made me *want* to make a purchase because I liked the people

I was reading about. Here's a sample of the style you might want to employ:

How Toot-Toot Model Train Village Began

I've been interested in Lionel electric trains ever since my brother and I received a set on Christmas Day 1953 from a cousin who was in the Air Force. Ever since then, trains have fascinated me.

My wife, Doris, and I actually met at a model train show at the Cow Palace in San Francisco, and were married six weeks later, so both of us have a keen interest in trains. Click here to see two of the train layouts we have in our recreation room.

Doris and I began Toot-Toot Model Train Village six years ago in a small store near our home in Fresno, California. We opened our Internet store (toot-toot-trains.com) in 1998, and since then we've outgrown our facilities twice. Our fair prices and huge selection have built a growing network of delighted hobbyists who come back again and again.

Feel free to e-mail us with your questions. We promptly answer all our e-mail and stand behind our products with a 100% No-Questions-Asked 60-Day Return Guarantee. But since our products are the finest quality and we take care to test everything before shipping, we've only had to make good on our guarantee three times in our six-year history.

We look forward to serving you and your train hobby.

Sincerely,
Herb and Doris Fitzmeyer
Toot-Toot Model Train Village

I realize that this sounds kind of hokey, but it builds trust. It has a way of bringing the shopper into a bit of the store owners' lives and their passion for trains. When the shopper is finished reading, he or she is much more ready to purchase from Herb and Doris than before. What they've said is believable and winsome. (Of course, you know that Herb and Doris Fitzmeyer and the Toot-Toot Model Train Village are imaginary! But don't you wish they were real?)

➤ Write in a Chatty Manner

Let the big companies write in their elevated, third-person, slightly snooty tone. You need to write in the same way you would talk to a shopper if he or she were directly across from you. It'll help you build a bond of friendship and trust that will produce sales.

➤ Display Testimonials from Satisfied Customers

As you develop satisfied customers, e-mail them and ask whether you can use for your promotional materials the kind words they've written. Nearly always they'll agree. Then excerpt two or three sentences for the testimonial. Make sure you use a variety of topics—one about your great customer service, another about your selection and prices, a third about how you took special time to explain something, a fourth about how they recommend your site to their friends, and a fifth about the promptness of your e-mails and shipping. Feel free to remove extraneous phrases or clauses from the final testimony, but make sure you don't change the wording or intent of the key items you leave in. Use full names with their permission, where they live, and ideally, a phone number to contact them. (Listing an e-mail address will subject your top customers to a barrage of spam.)

The personal touch is a powerful way to build trust.

■ An Ordering Policy That Builds Trust

For many years, Sears has clearly displayed its simple policy: "Satisfaction Guaranteed or Your Money Back." Do you think this policy has lost Sears money over the years? Hardly! It is one of the reasons people shop at Sears in the first place.

Small business store owners are often afraid to make strong, ironclad, no-questions-asked guarantees for fear that unscrupulous people will take advantage of them. And a few moral rejects *will* take advantage of them. But overwhelmingly, those who offer a money-back guarantee have found that it creates much more business than it causes problems.

➤ Risk Reversal

One of the reasons people hesitate to place an order in your store is the risk to which they feel they are exposing themselves. If you can reverse this so you the merchant take all the risk, and your customer takes none, you'll substantially increase the number of orders completed and expand your profit at the end of each month. Build trust by taking the risk on yourself.

➤ Ordering Policy Page

Make sure you have easy-to-find links all over your site to your ordering policy page. You'll need to include return policy, guarantee on products, and shipping policies.

Here are some examples of what to include in your policy page:

Drs. Foster & Smith (www.drsfostersmith.com/general/guarantee.cfm)

Amazon.com
  (www.amazon.com/exec/obidos/tg/browse/-/468532/
  ref=hy_f_4)

Lands' End (www.landsend.com/spawn.cgi?target=
  EDITGRTEXXXX)

The clearer you are, the more confidence you inspire. The more generous you are, the more trust you build. And remember, trust is the one essential business element you can't make sales without.

■ Associations That Build Trust

A final way to establish your business credibility is to associate your site with names known for their integrity. Each of these organizations requires some kind of investigation or accountability from you. In exchange for accountability and some money, you can use the organization's logo on your web site. Here are some to consider:

BBBOnline. The online version of the Better Business Bureau monitors how member businesses handle complaints, and provides a reference to consumers on what kinds of complaints have been registered. In addition to their "Reliability Seal" program, BBBOnline also offers a "Privacy Seal" for both kids' sites and general sites (www.bbbonline.com).

TRUSTe. Helps monitor privacy statements and policies (www.truste.com)

BizRate.com. After an online sale, buyers can rate the merchant on BizRate, and the aggregate of this rating scale is open to shoppers on the site (www.bizrate.com).

Exercise: List the ways you can improve your site so it builds trust more effectively.

Chapter *16*

Positioning Your Company in the Consumer's Mind

When someone hears your company's name (assuming they've heard of you), what kinds of associations do they make? What mental picture forms?

At the risk of you concluding that I am a few bricks short of a full load, I must confess that most Saturday nights I listen to Garrison Keillor's Prairie Home Companion (www .prairiehome.org) on Public Radio International. There—now you know. But I must quickly add that I listen to it to learn more about marketing in general, positioning in particular—and, of course, to laugh.

■ Prairie Home Companion

Two regulars to the show are Ralph's Pretty Good Grocery and The Ketchup Advisory Board. Ralph's Pretty Good Grocery can be found downtown in the mythical northern Minnesota town of Lake Wobegon. The name positions the store pretty clearly. It's not excellent, nor poor, nor gourmet, nor produce-only, but "pretty good." You may not have thought about it, but your online business has a place in the e-business pecking order, a certain position in people's minds. But if your company's "mind position" is only "pretty good," the chances are that visitors will never return. My dad, an art teacher, hung a sign in his classroom, "Mediocrity deserves no praise." Don't let "okay" or even "pretty good" define your site. You need something more.

Now to The Ketchup Advisory Board. Garrison Keillor's team writes different radio skits each week. Usually they involve a couple of people getting testy or downright unglued. Then one of them says, usually the wife, "Honey, maybe you need more ketchup. Its natural endorphins help you feel mellow." Then the theme song begins:

> These are the good years in the golden sun,
> A new day is dawning, a new life has begun . . .
> Love is flowing . . . like ketchup on a bun.

The announcer does a voiceover: "Ketchup. For the good times . . ." And the song fades off: "Ketchup . . . ketchup . . ."

I know it sounds pretty corny in print, but when you hear it on Saturday night, it makes you want to run down to the corner store—"What was the name of that grocery store, dear?"— and buy a bottle of thick, red ketchup. What Keillor has succeeded in doing is positioning ketchup among the foods, fruits, and vegetables that have hired ad agencies to represent them. How would you position ketchup with its natural endorphins, in relationship to orange juice that is said to prevent heart attacks? Or "the incredible, edible egg" or "pork, the other white meat" or "got milk?" or "beef . . . ," or dancing raisins, or any of the other foods vying for your attention?

■ Positioning Your Business

"Those industries spend millions of dollars to position themselves," I can hear you saying. "How can I position my business with little or no marketing budget to work with?" Very effectively, it turns out. All this relates closely to two concepts you've heard about before:

> *Unique Selling Proposition (USP):* It defines what makes your business unique from every other competitor in your field. It spells out the precise niche you seek to fill, and how you aim to fill it. If you can't tell who you are in two sentences, then your USP is too fuzzy to succeed.

> *Brand Name:* "Any word, 'device' (design, sound, shape, or color), or combination of these used to distinguish a seller's goods or services." (1)

The idea of a "brand" is bigger than the brand name itself. It is the feeling or impression the consumer has about your product evoked by seeing the product or the brand name. To produce this feeling or impression, marketers invest a great deal of energy—and often money. Let me give you an example in terms of retail store brands.

Set up a grid with four quadrants to help you understand your site in relationship to others (see Table 16.1).

Table 16.1   Positioning Grid

Kmart Low value added, high breadth	Nordstrom High value added, high breadth
Kinney Shoes Low value added, low breadth	Tiffany High value added, low breadth

The horizontal axis is "value added" (a high value added would include elements such as good location, reliability, prestige, etc.). The vertical axis is "breadth of product line" (narrow vs. broad). (2)

Other types of positioning grids might be Business Strength on one axis and Industry Attractiveness on the other. Or Market Growth vs. Market Share. Or Price vs. Quality, Customer Service vs. Price, or Convenience vs. Price. Select the axis names that help you clearly distinguish your position from competitors.

■ You've Got to Take a Stand

"Would you please describe the suspect you saw running from the convenience store?"

"Medium height and weight. Face was average. Hair color wasn't too dark, but it wasn't too light either."

"Age?"

"Middle-aged, I guess."

"What color were his clothes?"

"Oh, I don't know. They didn't really stand out."

The witness did a great job of identifying the suspect, didn't she?

Recently, I spoke on the phone with a vice president of a dot-com start-up. As he told me about his company, I immediately thought of other competing companies and mentioned one that's been getting a lot of media attention lately. "How do you compare your service in relation to Company X?" I asked, in as nonthreatening a way as possible.

He said, "We've studied that company, and they have a very good product."

Good start. Positioning yourself by running down your

competitors cheapens your company. I waited to see how he would position his new start-up.

"Well," he finally said, "if someone were to try Company X's product, and then try ours, I think they'd like ours better."

I was still waiting for a positioning statement. "Ours is easier to use for computer-phobic small businesspeople, and you can do more with it." Okay, finally a positioning statement that relates to ease of use. In all fairness, this new dot-com hasn't launched quite yet, and is still working out the final details. But unless they can instantly position themselves in relationship to their competitors in the public's mind, they have little chance of carving out their own market share. Here are some terms that are sometimes used in positioning statements:

Bigger

Easier to use

More capable

Highest quality Swiss steel

Unique engineering

Less expensive

Better service when you need it

More colorful

Makes a fashion statement

Will attract men's attention

Will make you wealthier

Will help you get out of debt more quickly

Faster acting

More nutritious

The most popular

Number one in customer satisfaction

You get the idea. You have to have something memorable, something that sets you apart, or you'll never rise high enough to be on anyone's radar. Positioning yourself clearly in the consumer's mind in relation to your competitors is absolutely vital. You don't have to mention your competitors by name, but you need to set yourself apart. One of my favorites is Michael Tchong's *Iconocast* newsletter (www .iconocast.com) that uses the tag line, "More concentrated than the leading brand."

■ Points of Difference

R.G. Cooper and E.J. Kleinschmidt studied 203 new industrial products to find the factors that most affected the product success rate. What they found was that having significant points of difference, a uniquely superior product, was most important. (3)

As you are very well aware, there is a lot of competition for which e-mail newsletters you'll actually read. In the area of marketing you'll find some excellent offerings, including *Iconocast*. When it came to positioning Doctor Ebiz (www .doctorebiz.com), I had to find some distinctives. Here's what I came up with:

Small business concerns vs. enterprise-level problems

Short and quickly read vs. long and time-consuming

Practical and focused on real problems vs. theoretical

Question-and-answer vs. articles

Weekly vs. daily or monthly

Free vs. paid subscription

I want to position Doctor Ebiz in the small businessperson's mind as the "Dear Abby of the e-business world." No single point of difference distinguishes *Doctor Ebiz,* but taken together, *Doctor Ebiz* is unique among e-mail newsletters. And because I have clearly defined its points of difference, I am able to market it much more effectively than if it were "Ralph's Pretty Good Newsletter."

What are the points of difference that make your product or service unique from your major competitors on the Web? With this knowledge you may not be able to overtake the leader, but you stand a good chance of carving out your own solid niche from which you can gradually increase market share.

With hard work and some ingenuity you might be able to reposition your business from a negative to a positive—such as from "a few bricks short of a full load" to "the spark of off-the-wall genius that sets him apart." Good luck.

Exercise: For your Internet Marketing Plan, write two paragraphs that list your company's points of difference, and then write one (or at the most, two) sentences that position your business, beginning with the words: "Our company holds a unique position on the Web in that we. . . ."

➤ References

1. Eric N. Berkowitz, Roger A. Kerin, Steven W. Hartley, and Richard D. Irwin, *Marketing* (fifth edition, Irwin, 1997), p. 329.
2. This retail-positioning matrix was developed by the MAC Group, Inc., a management-consulting firm, ibid., p. 482.
3. p. 299, cited from R.G. Cooper and E.J. Kleinschmidt, "New Products—What Separates Winners from Losers?," *Journal of Product Innovation Management* (Sept. 1987), pp. 169–184.

Part IV

The 4 Ps of Marketing

The 4 Ps of Marketing has been a standard way of describing marketing programs for 40 years. But do the 4 Ps work on the Internet? Yes, though differently than in traditional marketing.

If you've studied marketing in the 40-plus years since E. Jerome McCarthy originally wrote his classic *Basic Marketing,* then you're familiar with the 4 Ps of Marketing (speak only in hushed tones). It's a neat and memorable classification system of the various controllable elements of the marketing program portion of your Internet Marketing Plan. Here they are, focused on a particular target market or customer (Table IV.1).

Table IV.1   The 4 Ps of Marketing

Product	Individual goods, product lines, or services	Includes features, accessories, installation, instructions, service, warranty, packaging, and brand names
Place (distribution)	Getting the product to the customer	Channels, distribution systems, middlemen, warehousing, transportation, fulfillment, and shipping
Promotion	Communicating with the customer	Personal selling, mass selling, sales promotion, sales personnel, advertising, media selection, and copywriting
Price	Setting a price that serves the customer well and maximizes profits to the company	Price flexibility, level pricing, introductory pricing, discounts, allowances, and geographic terms

If you've been doing the exercises so far in this book, you know that developing your own Internet Marketing Plan takes considerable work to understand and characterize the market, the customer, and the environment in which you are doing business. The 4 Ps is a different part of the Plan. One way to look at this is uncontrollable factors vs. controllable factors.

Uncontrollable. The current economic environment includes elements such as consumer confidence, degree of unemployment, new technologies that threaten to displace your own, competitors that suddenly appear on the horizon, government regulations thought up by your favorite legislator, and changing consumer preferences. You can't control these.

Controllable. The 4 Ps represent elements of your marketing strategy that you *can* control. They depend upon such givens as your budget, personnel, and creativity, but you can do a lot to influence them.

As you write the Marketing Program section of your Internet Marketing Plan, you'll need to include a section for each of the 4 Ps that define your current marketing program. These are the four major ingredients of a traditional marketing mix directed at the customer or target market.

But are the 4 Ps really applicable to Internet marketing? The short answer is yes, with a few modifications. The following is an attempt to apply them to the typical situations faced by Web marketers today. Businesses vary so much that I can't be exhaustive, but only suggestive, as we examine each.

Chapter

17

P1—Product Strategy

Let's understand what a product is in Internet space so you can plan how to market it.

The first P in the 4 Ps of Marketing is *product*. Except for manufacturers, for many businesses the product strategy part of marketing is really about marketing the company, often not the individual goods or services that the company offers. So as we discuss product marketing strategy, begin to think of your business as the product you are marketing, and you'll gain some new insights.

■ Various Product Factors

Of course, there is much overlap in aspects of an Internet Marketing Plan. Various sections look at some of the same realities in different ways. In Chapter 16, for example, we discussed points of difference and positioning. These relate both to your business and to your line of products or services.

Branding also concerns product strategies, though we won't discuss it in this chapter. There's more information on branding at www.wilsonweb.com/cat/cat.cfm?page = 1&subcat = ma _Branding.

Other product strategy items include your guarantee and customer service policies to support the product, instructions on how to install and use the product or service, and product accessories. Troubleshooting trees, knowledge bases, and FAQs that support the product or service are also part of your product marketing strategy.

■ Packaging

On grocery store shelves, packaging has a lot to do with which box of cereal you select. On the Web, however, packaging doesn't work the same way, since site selection is often made on the basis of search engines or traditional advertising. On the Internet the packaging comes after the initial advertisement, and consists of web site design elements that create a stimulating selling environment using color and graphics. (See "12 Ways to Give Your Webstore a Sales Boost," www.wilsonweb.com/ebooks/sales-boost.htm.) Of course, web site packaging can be projected to your customers via HTML e-mail in order to draw your previous customer back into your store.

■ The Product You Market Is Often the Web Site

As I mentioned, for many companies, the product you are marketing *is* the company itself, the business. Yes, you may be talking about individual products among your products or services, but your overall message is, "Buy it at our site for these reasons. . . . Let us serve you because. . . ." As we discuss various kinds of Web businesses, you can see this interplay of marketing the web site product as well as your goods or services products.

■ Kinds of Internet Products or Companies

Manufactured goods. If you're a manufacturer, then your products are self-evident. Your business probably isn't General Motors, but you may be among the many small manufacturers on the Web. Perhaps you're an artist or woodworker selling your creations. You may have a tool-and-die shop that produces custom parts according to specific customer needs (so you're probably marketing more of a service than goods). You may have a single product or a product line you are producing or importing. But usually you're advertising your company on the Web, not an individual product by itself. You want the online community to know and visit your web site. Getting your business known is the major goal of your marketing for now. (Of course, there are exceptions to this.)

Online catalogs. Web catalog sites are essentially wholesale or retail order-taking terminals. They may carry products from dozens or thousands of manufacturers. But what is the product? Their own store is the product here. They are building an online brand that they hope will represent to you the kind of store where you can find and purchase just what you want. Yes, they market their product lines through HTML e-mail fliers, but they're essentially saying, "Come here, come to our store out of all the other choices on the Web. We have what you're looking for." One way to look at an online catalog site is as a shopping service that helps you find what you want among their carefully selected collection of best-of-class products.

Amazon.com is an example you may be familiar with, but how about free catalogs? One early software download site is www.Tucows.com. What is their service? Storage and download of thousands of shareware software programs. Tucows.com offers a vast product line, though none of their products are unique to Tucows.com. But the site itself is unique in the way it is arranged, in its breadth of offerings, in the software reviews it carries, in the speed of its servers, and in the geographic diversity of its server locations. Online catalogs offer a branded shopping service. (Of course, there's more, but I am simplifying.)

Online services. In a similar way, many online services can be thought of and marketed as products, too. HitBox .com, for example, offers a suite of services for the webmaster to check your spelling, analyze the accuracy of your HTML code, score your META tags (invisible keywords and a description that help search engines index your site), track visitors to your pages, and generally massage and clean up your web site. You can find service sites that will calculate your taxes; others predict your success, personal characteristics, and love prospects based on your birth date and relative planetary positions in the heavens. Web sites compare prices of computer monitors available at other online businesses. Search engines are really an online service, and the list goes on. Think of your site's collection of services as the product you are marketing.

Custom services. Custom services, too, can be viewed as products. In the mid-90s I pioneered marketing web site and e-commerce design services as product packages. One of the keys to success was defining the standard product carefully, clarifying what was included in the standard web site, and identifying which items were considered add-ons. I learned to market not just a web site, but a 12-page web site that included a single response form, custom graphic header, background, menu system, and certain marketing elements. When you package your services into clearly defined bundles, they become a product that is recognizable to the customer and therefore salable. Your service packages constitute your product line.

Information products. One of my favorite sites is www. Britannica.com, the web site that includes the entire *Encyclopedia Britannica*. What a wealth of material—a great example of an information product. An online newspaper is another example of an information product, as well as our E-Commerce Research Room (www.wilsonweb.com/research). So is *Doctor Ebiz* (www.doctorebiz.com)—a question-and-answer e-mail newsletter designed to help small businesses solve their problems.

Entertainment products. Very close to information products are entertainment sites—online games, music, and photo essays, among others.

■ Price Tag Is Irrelevant

Often we don't view a site as a product because we are offering something to consumers for free. Don't let the price tag or lack of it fool you. Think of your web site as a product, and your content as product lines, and you'll know how better to market.

You must make money somewhere, of course. A common Internet strategy is to offer some information products or services free, and then charge for others. Often you are marketing the free products to attract people to your site, and the for-fee products to site visitors who are drawn by your free offers.

The exception, of course, is if you have no product at all. I've seen a lot of product-less sites on Yahoo! GeoCities. Here's a typical site: me, a photo of my apartment, a picture of my girlfriend with me at the beach last year, my pet peeves, my peevish pet, my favorite hobbies. Oh, and a few affiliate program banners I wish you would click on in order to make me wealthy without working.

If you want a business that earns money, if you want to attract significant traffic, then you must offer a web site product that customers want. Seeing your web site as a product in and of itself enables you to market it more effectively.

■ Your Product Strategy

Your online business becomes more attractive as you add related products and product lines that appeal to your customers.

Let's say you sell a nutritional supplement that encourages muscle growth. Who is buying this? Weight lifters and college athletes, you determine. What similar products would interest them? Perhaps three concentrated strengths of your products. Perhaps a line of natural soothing treatments for sore muscles—you get the idea. Look for a mix of products that will appeal to your customers. Perhaps you'll offer "better" and "best" lines that allow you to upsell.

Don't try to do too much too quickly, but plan to introduce new products that fit your overall product strategy.

Exercise: Define the overall product that your web site offers. The richer the product-set the more attractive your business. Now describe your product strategy, that is, the way you are planning for your products or services to complement each other and stimulate sales.

Chapter 18

P2—Place (Distribution)

Here are the advantages and disadvantages of three different Internet retail distribution models: drop-shipping, inventory, and fulfillment house. You might be surprised by which will turn out to be the best for you.

If you've done much speaking you know that speakers love alliteration, that is, making each of the points of the speech start with the same letter. The problem is that in order to make everything fit, you may have to squeeze some of the points a bit. They just don't quite work. But the speech must go on. You pull out a thesaurus, grit your teeth, find a shoehorn, and *make* it fit. I think that's what happened when E. Jerome McCarthy came up with his 4 Ps of Marketing. Product, promotion, and price are all self-explanatory. But place? What does it mean? What does geography have to do with it?

Place is supposed to signify the physical distribution channel, getting the goods to the customer. Yes, the Internet is either the point of contact or the point of sale, but the *failure* to consider the distribution channel dooms many online businesses. Of course, if you offer a digital product, such as entertainment, information, or software, you may be able to distribute electronically via the Web, e-mail, or file download, eliminating the need for any other distribution system and keeping costs very low. Unfortunately, the world needs more than information, entertainment, and software. Services are typically delivered digitally online or, with the Internet, used to generate leads, with the service being delivered in person by a local vendor. In this chapter we're looking primarily at distributing nondigital products.

■ Meet Bob

"Internet product sales are easy," said Bob Simple when he first set up Bob Simple's Online Shoes. Now he's not so sure. He had found three quality shoe manufacturers who agreed to ship shoes to his customers as soon as he faxed them the order. What's more, the manufacturers used Bob's labels and included his completed order form in the box as a packing slip. "Slam dunk," said Bob Simple. "I don't have to invest in any inventory, the manufacturers have hundreds of hard-to-find sizes that I can advertise. My costs are minimal."

■ Drop-Shipping Model

Bob Simple had bought into the drop-shipping model, as have tens of thousands of online stores. And they have found thousands of willing manufacturers and distributors who are glad for the opportunity to sell more of their products. We profiled this approach in *Web Commerce Today*, November 15, 1998, Issue 16 (www.wilsonweb.com/wct2/issue16.htm).

You'll find some catalogs of drop-shipper manufacturers and distributors, and other resources, in that issue (http://www .wilsonweb.com/wct2/981115drop-ship-resources.htm).

Drop-shipping has some very strong advantages and a few disadvantages. Let's look at the advantages first.

No inventory costs. Purchasing product inventory that is ready to ship to your purchasers is expensive. In addition to the out-of-pocket costs, you need a place to store the inventory. Finally, you have to pick, pull, pack, and ship the products once the order is placed. Having the distributor or manufacturer take on all these costs and responsibilities lifts a real burden off your shoulders.

Drop-shipper is transparent. With most of your drop-shippers, especially those with whom you do a regular business, you can send them labels and forms so their package looks like it is from you. Your customer probably won't know that your hands never touched the product.

It almost sounds too good to be true. But there are two major problems:

Lower margins. While the manufacturer may be willing to sell you its product for 30% to 40% of suggested retail, expect to see another 10% or so off your margins if you want drop-shipping services. On the Internet, some categories of products are very price-sensitive, and often the street price is substantially under the suggested retail price. For example, if you're selling computer hardware using the drop-shipping model, you may find it hard to be competitive price-wise and still make a profit. The difference between making money and losing it may be only a few percent. Unless you're very careful, drop-shipping may put you out of business.

Crippled customer service. Let me tell you a story. For too many years I squinted at a 14-inch monitor. Finally I decided to get a 19-inch monitor that won *PC Magazine* Editor's Choice recognition. I went to Egghead (www.egghead.com), probably because my family says that my head looks much like the old Egghead mascot of brick-and-mortar days. I found the monitor, and it indicated the ability to ship soon, so I ordered it. Immediately I got an e-mail that said the monitor was back-ordered. Why didn't they tell me that before I ordered? I was ticked off, but decided to give them a while—after all, it could come any time. So I waited, visions of a shiny new 19-inch monitor dancing in my head. After a week with no word, I finally got tired of waiting and called customer service. I was connected to a polite customer service person who listened to my question:

"When will the monitor be available?"

"We don't know, sir. The manufacturer hasn't told us."

I was frustrated. I had looked around and *knew* it was in stock at another company. "Cancel the order, then," I told the lady, impatiently.

"You have to give 72 hours notice before canceling," she said.

"That's just unacceptable," I retorted. "If you don't have the monitor ready to ship now, then cancel it."

"The manufacturer may be ready to ship it."

Aha! I thought. This is a drop-shipping operation. "Then call the manufacturer and ask, please," I told her.

"I can't do that, sir."

"Then cancel the order. Now!" I was disgusted.

She cancelled the order. The next day the monitor arrived by next-day courier. It had been shipped, but Egghead's communication with the manufacturer was such that Egghead didn't know what was going on.

In the meantime, I had ordered the monitor from another dealer, and subsequently returned the monitor from Egghead. Why did the Egghead site show the item in stock when it wasn't? Probably because the inventory available wasn't updated in real time, or often enough to be accurate. (To be fair, Egghead's communication with its drop-shippers has improved since then, and I still order through them.)

Lesson: Drop-shipping may well handicap your ability to provide excellent customer service. And without excellent customer service, you'll lose your best customers to your competitors. If price doesn't distinguish you from other online businesses, then customer service most certainly must. Though I've had one occasion to return a book to Amazon, I go back loyally because when I called about the problem they handled it so very well.

■ Local Distributor Model

After receiving a day's orders, the e-tailer purchases the products from a local distributor, and then transports them to their own facility for packing and shipping. This was Amazon.com's original method of fulfillment when it was small, using an Ingram book distribution outlet in the same city. The method only works where the distributor can keep an adequate stock on hand that the e-tailer can obtain quickly. The advantage is that the e-tailer doesn't have capital tied up in inventory or unneeded warehouse space, has all the shipping records on hand, and has a good idea of the distributor's stock. The disadvantage is that the e-tailer is very dependent upon distributors' supplies, and may not be able to accurately reflect available inventory to shoppers before they purchase.

■ Inventory Model

The tried-and-true retail method is to order an item from the manufacturer or distributor and keep it in stock until you receive an order. This has some advantages:

You can ship immediately. The faster you can turn around the order, the more impressed your customer is, and the better chance you have of getting him or her back the next time.

You can provide excellent customer service. In case of a problem, you will have all the records at your fingertips to trace the order and make a correction. In the online book wars, Amazon.com invested a great deal of money building regional warehouses and buying a share in a same-day Manhattan courier firm to enable it to provide excellent customer service. As a result, they will be very hard to beat, though early on they don't show a profit because of the huge initial investment.

Inventory, of course, has its disadvantages, too:

Prepaid inventory can sit on your shelves, tying up capital. Amazon.com overestimated the number of orders for Christmas 1999, and had too much inventory at the beginning of January. When you own the inventory, you also own the risk. If a product doesn't sell, you're stuck with disposing of it at pennies on the dollar.

You must have an efficient fulfillment system. One of the reasons that brick-and-mortar stores are slow on the uptake when it comes to online business is that retail store supply is done with a pallet-size logistical system. A regional warehouse is designed to ship pallet loads to area stores. But Internet retail requires an entirely different kind of fulfillment system. Internet retail is essentially mail order, with shipments going out in parcel sizes to end users. Few brick-and-mortar retailers have a humming mail order business to draw experience from and are starting from scratch with an entirely different kind of fulfillment system. An inefficient fulfillment system can lose for you the advantages in good customer service that holding the inventory gained for you. An inefficient fulfillment system eats into profit margins.

■ Fulfillment House

A third common Internet distribution model is the fulfillment house (actually a subset of the inventory model). A fulfillment house, the offspring of the direct marketing industry, will handle some or all of the aspects of getting the product to your customer. They will maintain inventory, order new product, assemble, pick, pull, pack, and ship, all according to your specifications and with your labels. They will also handle the order taking, the Internet shopping cart, and provide an ordering and customer service call center if you need one. In other words, you can run an entirely virtual business, outsourcing everything to the fulfillment house, if you like. Of course, they take their pound of flesh. I think this works best for proprietary products—products with a higher than average margin. But if you have a single product, such as a book or tape series, using a fulfillment house will probably be preferable to having stacks of products lining the halls of your home. You can find fulfillment houses in the "Yellow Pages" section of DM News (www .dmnews.com/) or in Yahoo's "Fulfillment Services" category. A service that caters to the needs of small Internet start-ups is Paul Purdue's iFulfill.com in Dundee, Michigan (www.ifulfill.com).

Which of these three models should you use? No one can make that decision for you. But armed with the pros and cons, you'll be able to make a thoughtful choice that will leverage the advantages and minimize the disadvantages of one of these models, and include it as part of your Internet Marketing Plan.

Exercise: Describe the fulfillment model you have selected and why, then explain how you will mitigate its disadvantages.

■ Crucial Differences between Retailing and E-Tailing

The retail business model that is practiced in thousands of shops and strip malls in cities all over the world is widely understood. However, many fail to understand that the Internet e-tail business model is substantially different. Some of these differences are obvious, while others become clear only later—sometimes only when it is difficult to respond to them. Here are the differences I see, along with the barriers and benefits found in an online store business model.

➤ Retail versus Mail Order

The retail model involves leasing a display room and ordering products into inventory which are stocked on display shelves. Shopping is either do-it-yourself or salesperson-assisted. Goods are purchased at a cash register, packed in plastic bags, and carried out with the customer. The e-tailing model, on the other hand, has much more in common with catalog mail-order sales than with retail. Customers shop with little assistance in an online storefront, pay via credit card, and products are shipped or drop-shipped to them via a parcel courier or postal carrier. When you think about it, the business models are really very different. Let's look at the contrast between these models a bit more carefully.

➤ Shopping—Tactile versus Non-Tactile

Retail stores allow shoppers to see and touch the products, to make sure they are getting what they want. Shelves carry boxes containing products; shoppers read product information on the box, and perhaps open the box to examine the contents. Usually a shopper can ask questions of a store clerk, while in some stores salespeople actively try to assist.

Online stores, however, only allow the shopper to look at pictures and read product information. The best online stores, though, are able to provide more product information online than a retail shopper might find. Sometimes this wealth of information can make up for the absence of a salesperson. But the better stores are providing some kind of live chat or instant phone call to answer questions. While retail shoppers can see and personally examine the product before purchasing, online stores need to make special efforts to help shoppers get what they want, or face expensive product returns after delivery.

➤ Market Scope and Competition

The competition that retail stores face is mainly from other stores within driving distance. It may be fierce on the local front, but at least the number of competing stores is finite. For online stores, on the other hand, the competition can seem almost infinite. Since geographic barriers pose little limitation to shoppers, an online store is forced to compete with every other similar online store in the entire country, and, at least in some niches, with all similar stores globally. The competition online is indeed staggering. It is difficult to rise above the clutter to even be noticed, and the store's position on search engines may be buried beneath 20 or 30 others.

But before you despair, realize that the vastness of the Internet is also its great strength. Instead of just relying on a customer base within driving distance, your customers can come literally from your entire nation, and, to some degree, from around the world wherever your language is spoken. Yes, the competition is great, but the market is absolutely huge. With good marketing, a local store might be nicely profitable, but a well-marketed online store could serve a much larger clientele and earn huge profits.

The key for the online store owner is to find and perfect a marketing mix that is within budget, but also effective in bringing in customers. Though the competition seems intense, if you poke and prod just a bit, you find that most of the competition is flabby. Their storefronts are a sham, the lights are on but nobody is home, and the store owners aren't working very hard or have given up. If you work both smart and hard, you can conceivably carve out a substantial slice of business within your niche, despite the competition. On balance, I would rather have lots of competitors and still have access to a huge market, than limit both, since entrepreneurial skills can move a business toward the top.

➤ Inventory and Real Estate Costs

The typical retail store business model requires several thousand square feet for inventory displayed in a pleasing manner on shelves, a checkout stand, and a backroom for extra inventory. And since the retailer is trying to attract walk-in traffic, this real estate must be zoned commercial, requiring high lease costs per square foot.

E-tailers, on the other hand, since they never meet the public face-to-face, can occupy space in a home office, a garage, less expensive office space, or lower-cost light industrial warehouse space. This saves substantial overhead.

No matter the differences in the models, however, there remains the need for inventory space. As we have mentioned, e-tailers meet this need in one of four ways: warehouse inventory, local distributor, drop-shipping, and fulfillment houses.

■ Fulfillment Costs

Retailers provide product fulfillment to their customers by stocking shelves, providing shopping carts with real (not virtual) wheels, checkout stands, and plastic bags in which shoppers carry purchases to their cars. E-tailers' costs include shipping department employees, boxes, tape, internal packing, shipping costs (usually passed on to the customer), and order tracking.

Of course, fulfillment costs are closely related to the inventory method selected. If you carry inventory in-house and have your own shipping department, you are betting that costs will be lower this way than outsourcing to companies that are set up to do this very efficiently. Many analysts believe that fulfillment costs, along with customer acquisition costs, will determine whether an online store can stay in business. This is a big, unseen, e-commerce key. The more efficient your shipping operation, the better your overall profit margin. The more time and money consumed by inefficient operations, the more likely you are to fail.

➤ Customer Service Costs and Returned Goods

Closely related to the method of fulfillment you choose is the level of customer service you can provide. Smaller retail stores designate one or two key employees who handle time-consuming customer inquiries, complaints, and returns. Larger stores have a customer service desk where customer service inquiries are handled. There is no money to be made here. In fact, bins behind the customer service counter contain many returned items that are a drain on profits. The purpose, however, is to retain customer confidence and good will. Smart retailers follow the dictum that the customer is always right—even when he is wrong. Displeased customers can easily decide to both (1) never shop in the store again, and (2) tell several others how badly they were treated. Customer trust is ground-zero for business success.

E-tailers often neglect customer service. The large e-tailers learned the miseries of poor customer service during Christmas 1999. But many smaller e-tailers have yet to take customer service seriously. Instead of a customer service desk, e-tailers usually provide a customer service e-mail address. Smarter e-tailers provide a telephone number where dissatisfied customers can quickly speak to a real person. Live chat can also provide instant real-person attention. Customer service can sometimes be outsourced to call centers or fulfillment houses. But great customer service is the second big key to e-tailing success. Since customers are so expensive to acquire, to make any money, existing customers must be retained at whatever cost—since that cost is very likely to be lower than customer acquisition costs.

► Customer Acquisition and Retention Costs

The customer acquisition cost is a very important figure to retailers and e-tailers. It is based on the total cost a company spends on advertising and marketing promotions divided by the total number of new customers obtained through that spending. If a retailer spends $2,500 on a newspaper display ad that brings about 300 customers into his or her store over the weekend, and 65% of them make a purchase, the customer acquisition cost is $12.82 [$2,500/(300 * .65) = $12.82]. An e-tailer that spends $2,500 for keyword banner advertising on Yahoo! may purchase 100,000 impressions. A 2% click-through rate brings 2,000 shoppers, and a 5% conversion rate (percentage of buyers to shoppers) means that 100 will make purchases, producing a customer acquisition cost of $25 [$2,500/(100,000 * .02 * .05) = $25].

One difference between retail and e-tail is the rather low conversion rate in online stores compared to their brick-and-mortar cousins (though my 65% conversion rate for retail stores is just a guess). Another difference is the relatively high customer acquisition costs for online stores. Here were some 1998–1999 acquisition costs (http://internet.miningco.com/ industry/internet/library/weekly/1999/aa123099a.htm) (Table 18.1).

Table 18.1   Some Customer Acquisition Costs
for Online Stores

Company/Business	Acquisition Cost
Amazon.com	$29
Various e-commerce sites	$34
Ameritrade	$178
DLJ Direct	$185
E*Trade	$257
Credit cards	$50–$75
Mortgage lenders	$100–$250

The implications of these staggering amounts compared to the average customer's initial purchase mean that many e-tailers who advertise regularly will lose money on a customer's first sale. The only way e-tailers can recoup these losses is by retaining customers and selling to them again and again.

If customer acquisition costs are bad news for e-tailers, customer retention costs should come as good news. Once you have a happy online customer, you also have an e-mail address in your customer database, and know something about his or her interests. If you can leverage this database to produce e-mail messages every few weeks, then you can build the relationship and encourage the customer to come back for additional purchases at a very low-cost advertising cost.

Larger businesses must invest hundreds of thousands of dollars in CRM (customer relationship management) software, but small e-tailers may be able to do this by downloading order information into a Microsoft Access database and then using queries to produce select lists to which targeted e-mails can be sent via an e-mail merge program according to the type of product previously purchased, for example. Several lower-cost systems are available. You can use other Microsoft Office products (Access, Outlook, and Word), MessageMedia's Mail-

King software (www.messagemedia.com/solutions/mailking), or Gammadyne Mailer (www.gammadyne.com/mmail.htm). If you don't need to be quite so precise, you can always e-mail specials and sales to your entire customer list for only pennies per message (or nothing, if you don't count the value of your time).

The lesson here is that e-tailers *must* retain their customers and sell to them again and again if they are to make a profit. Those that sell a few high-margin products may not need repeat customers, but e-tail storeowners with average margins *must* retain customers and find inexpensive ways to market to them.

➤ Sales Taxes

In these early days of the Internet in the United States we've had a moratorium on new Internet sales taxes, and online businesses have flourished as a result. But state governors have become increasingly restive when they see Internet companies locate in states without sales taxes or offshore tax havens and then sell to consumers in states with sales taxes. Currently, U.S. law requires companies with a corporate or physical presence in a state or states to collect sales taxes from residents of those states only. But I don't think this will last. I expect to see laws requiring Internet merchants to collect appropriate state sales taxes from each of their U.S. customers, and remit that tax to the respective state government. This will have three effects: (1) tax calculation will increasingly be outsourced to companies like Taxware.com (www.taxware.com), (2) paperwork could become excessive so merchants will outsource tax collection and distribution to third-party firms, and (3) consumers won't have the same incentive as before to purchase online. End-user prices on the Internet will no longer look so attractive. I don't look forward to this, but I see it coming.

➤ Staffing Costs

The retail industry typically pays salesclerks low wages. E-tailers have the advantage of being able to locate in low-wage areas, or outsource to virtual workers in low-wage areas. But virtual workers typically possess computer equipment and skills that allow them to demand higher wages, especially as contract workers (in contrast to employees). But e-tailers don't need cashiers, since online shoppers complete their own sales transactions unaided. Customer service and fulfillment personnel are still needed, however. All but the smallest e-tailers will need to keep their staffs lean in order to stay competitive.

➤ Start-up Costs

While brick-and-mortar retailers may have difficulty opening a small store for less than $50,000 in inventory, furnishings, signage, lease, etc., the small e-tailer can often set up shop for 10% to 20% of that amount or less, then grow as profits make growth feasible.

Many of the larger dot-coms have spent millions on computer infrastructure, custom programming, and in-house servers. Smaller e-tailers, however, can often outsource e-commerce hosting for $40 to $400 per month and often purchase "off-the-shelf" e-commerce software that includes most or all of the capabilities they need. Compared to a retail store, a mom-and-pop online store can be set up on a shoestring, and run very profitably as a family business.

➤ The Bottom Line

The reason I've compared retail and e-tail is to help dispel the myth that e-tailing is just like retailing but without the hassles. The differences between retail and e-tail are significant, and you must thoroughly understand them in order to stay in business. True, e-tailing can cut start-up investment, as well as some sales and marketing costs. But in the final analysis the basic business rules still apply. E-tailing is *not* easy. To make a profit you must get several crucial elements right:

- Excellent customer service that delights customers and retains them for future sales.
- Repeat sales from existing customers at low incremental advertising costs.
- A reasonable customer acquisition cost that drives an adequate number of first-time sales.
- A product fulfillment system that keeps fulfillment costs low and enables excellent customer service.

■ How Realistic Is an Online Store as an Add-on to a Retail Store?

In the struggle between "pure-play" Web-only e-tailers and the established brick-and-mortar retailers (sometimes called "click-and-mortar" stores), the latter are now going online in earnest and seem to be gaining.

➤ Advantages of Click-and-Mortar Retailers

National retail chains now seem to be taking to the Web, but for the longest time they were biding their time. National retailers have several advantages:

A *recognizable national brand.* They don't have to build their brand from scratch like Web-only companies. They already possess built-in trust and customer loyalty.

An established company. For national retailers, the Web is not a make-it-or-break-it proposition. They have the capital to continue until it becomes profitable.

Excellent customer service. If national retailers can deliver customer service to online customers in their retail stores, they can offer a level of service that Web-only e-tailers are unable to reproduce.

But national retailers have some struggles, too.

Learning curve. Retail is a lot different from e-tailing, which is essentially a mail-order catalog business. National retailers have to master an entirely new kind of business in order to succeed.

Logistics are different. Most retail chains are set up to distribute products from warehouses to stores in pallet-size loads. E-tailing requires distributing products to end users in package-size containers. Very different!

Expensive servers and software. National retailers don't have the luxury of starting small with outsourced e-commerce hosting. They are working on such a large scale that they need to go to the expense of building a system that will take a lot of traffic without failure.

Integration. Integrating Internet customer, inventory, and product databases with existing company databases is complex and expensive. But without integration, much of the power the system is capable of can't be realized.

Investment costs. Many national retailers have found they must form separate companies for their online incarnations for two reasons. First, the personnel need different skills and a different mindset than traditional retailers. Second, investment in a separate company can be treated for accounting purposes as a capital investment rather than an operating loss.

➤ Advantages of Pure-Play E-Tailers

Pure-play, Web-only e-tailers have some advantages, too, such as:

Flexibility. They are small enough to learn quickly and make necessary changes.

Understanding. They live and breathe the Internet, working in their own medium.

Costs. Pure-play e-tailers aren't burdened with huge capital investments in prime-location real estate and buildings. If they can keep costs down, they can compete successfully with their established competitors.

But it is becoming clear that there are many disadvantages. To name a couple:

Branding. Pure-plays must spend a great deal of money paying for brand recognition that click-and-mortar businesses already possess.

Funding. Many pure-play e-tailers have gone through their first and second rounds of funding, and still aren't profitable, so further funding is drying up.

➤ Advantages of Mom-and-Pop Click-and-Mortar Businesses

I think that mom-and-pop retailers have an excellent chance of profiting from adding an e-commerce department to their existing retail operation. Advantages are:

Start-up costs. Initial costs are relatively low. E-commerce hosting can be outsourced. The main expense is creating a product database with full product information and product photos to be uploaded to the online store.

Inventory. Since the mom-and-pop store already carries the products in stock, it can sell from the same inventory it manages for its retail business.

Customer service. Since inventory and shipping are done in-house, customer service can be quick, efficient, and personal. A telephone can be installed to reach an employee who is assigned part-time, and later full-time, to the e-commerce department.

Shipping. Shipping will be a new operation for a retailer, but a relatively small shipping operation can be conducted with part-time help from the back room of a retail shop.

I believe that a mom-and-pop retailer can add 10% to 30% to annual revenue from an online store rather easily so that profits show up quickly. The biggest challenge I see is growth. If the online department flourishes, it will outgrow the existing brick-and-mortar location, along with most of the built-in advantages that come with it. A new location, new employees, and new accounting and inventory programs must be set up, cutting into profitability. So long as the online department is relatively small, it can be a rather easy, low-risk, and profitable addition to the overall business.

■ Decision: Distribution Chain Strategies in the Internet Age

Long, long ago in a galaxy far, far away, things were orderly, following rules that had existed for ages. Goods were passed from manufacturers to end users in carefully constructed distribution chains that looked something like this:

Manufacturer → Wholesaler/Distributor → Retailer →
End User

Then came an alien race of Internet entrepreneurs who reinvented the distribution chain, skipping the intermediate layers, and causing "disintermediation" (in case you needed a great word to impress your boss with). These earthlings called the process by the strange idiom "upsetting the apple-cart." One of these applecart-upsetters was Dell Computer Corporation. Since they didn't have any existing distribution system to protect, they went direct:

Manufacturer → End User

This threw the IBMs and Compaq Computers of this world into a tizzy. Should they sell direct, too? Could they afford to alienate the distribution system they had so carefully put together? Or is Dell's operation still pretty small? Maybe this won't affect our business that much. Wrong. Dell is now the top manufacturer of PCs, leaving the competition in the dust. Since they do not need to allow two levels of price markups, they can afford to offer computers to end users at lower prices and still maintain a good margin. To save even more money, they don't manufacture the computers until they are ordered, saving the costs of inventory storage for finished goods. Tough competition.

Dell's example, among others, is causing great pain to manufacturers and their middlemen. Can they afford to sell directly? Can they afford not to? Here are the five most common ways that businesses are dealing with the distribution chain disruption caused by the Internet:

- *No sales on the Internet.* Web site points to retail stores only. Example: Thomasville furniture (www.thomasville .com)

- *No sales from company site.* Points to online and physical stores. Example: HarperCollins publishers (www.harpercollins.com)

- *Sales on Internet pay commissions to regional sales organizations.* Example: IBM (www.ibm.com) and Ethan Allen furniture (www.ethanallen.com)

- *Sales on the Internet are at list prices only.* Retailers are allowed to discount prices. Example: John Wiley & Sons publishers (www.wiley.com)

- *Direct sales on the Internet to end users.* No middlemen. Example: Dell Computer Corp. (www.dell.com)

It remains to be seen which models will survive over the long term—that is, which models allow manufacturers to be competitive at the same time as providing excellent customer service to end users.

Exercise: If you are a manufacturer, which of these distribution models will you use? Of course, if you're a Web-only company, you'll be using #5. But if you were an existing business in pre-Internet days, chances are you'll be looking at #1 through #4. Make this explicit in your Internet Marketing Plan.

■ Decision: Selecting Shipping Services

Most Internet merchants have two main choices for shipping products to end users, postal service—US Postal Service, Royal Mail, etc., and courier service—FedEx, UPS, Airborne, etc.

In order to stay competitive you need to balance two customer needs against each other: speedy delivery and inexpensive delivery.

One of the mistakes that some Internet merchants have made is to assume that all customers would rather pay more for courier delivery than to accept less expensive, but slower, postal delivery. In the United States, delivery confirmation enables merchants to prove that packages have been delivered, making postal service much more attractive for order fulfillment than before. My recommendation: Offer your customers the choice of overnight, second-day, ground, or postal delivery. That way you can stay competitive on price *and* let your customers decide how important shipping costs are to them.

Exercise: Write down your shipping strategy as part of the "place" portion of your Internet Marketing Plan.

Chapter 19

P3—Promotion

If you are confused by all the different methods of web site promotion, this chapter will help you make sense out of the basic types.

What are the foundational principles of promotion? I've come up with five. Only five.

■ The Five Mutable Laws of Web Marketing

This is embarrassing. Al Ries and Jack Trout have their *22 Immutable Laws of Marketing* (HarperBusiness, 1994), and what do I offer? Five measly laws, and mine are mutable, flexible, still growing and changing. But they form the backbone of present-day Web marketing lore, so I'll share them with you. And when they become immutable, you'll be the first to know. Trust me. They are: The Law of the Dead-End Street, The Law of Giving and Selling, The Law of Trust, The Law of Pull and Push, and The Law of the Niche.

➤ 1. The Law of the Dead-End Street

The first law goes like this: *Setting up a web site is like building a storefront on a dead-end street. If you want any shoppers, you must give them a reason to come.*

You've heard, too many times, "If you build it, they will come." We know that doesn't work on the Internet. But why do novices again and again build web sites without the least thought to a viable marketing plan? Maybe it's because FrontPage promises you a "professional looking site" and Microsoft hasn't yet offered WebMarket 2002. (Don't worry, they probably will pretty soon. Hi, Bill!)

The most wonderful site in the world is wasted unless people stop by to admire and purchase. It's the same reason that most great craftsmen aren't millionaires; they've learned to make a great product, but don't have a clue about marketing.

So the first question you need to ask yourself, even before you build your company's site, is: How will we get people to visit? Perhaps your marketing plan will look like this:

- Banner ads for two months to boost name recognition.
- Search engine positioning on HotBot and Excite in the first quarter, to include Infoseek, Lycos, and AltaVista in the second quarter.
- Reciprocal links with our industry organization and a paid listing in their directory.
- A newsworthy contest in the third quarter, for which we'll try to get full media coverage through press releases and calls from a PR agency.
- A company newsletter that carries industry news rather than just company drivel, to begin in the fourth quarter (though you should start collecting e-mail addresses now).

Then decide which of these activities to carry out in-house and which to outsource, attach a dollar value to each, and provide for them in your marketing budget. Your marketing plan may look much different than this, but you must give visitors a reason to come.

Many sites I visit are pretty slim. Yes, they give information about the company and its services, but nothing you'd want to bookmark. What compelling content can you put on your site that will make someone want to return? Content is primary.

With excellent content, when you ask for a reciprocal link, you don't have to plead, "Link to us because we're the greatest." You can say, "Link to us because we offer everything a buyer needs to know to select the right lighting fixture." When you offer a public service, you suddenly become newsworthy. Trade journals and magazines begin to mention you, and traffic follows. Give visitors a reason to come, and they will.

➤ 2. The Law of Giving and Selling

An important element of Web culture is free stuff. The Law of Giving and Selling says: *Attract visitors to your site by giving away something free, and then try to sell something additional to those who visit.*

You've seen this scenario played out in countless brick-and-mortar stores. "Free wool scarves to the first 50 people who visit our store for our annual One-Day Ski Sale on December 1." Give them something free, then try to sell them something.

Here's how we used this strategy. In mid-1995 Wilson Internet Services launched a web site design business with a goal of attracting business nationally via the Web. At that time even *local* web site designers were considered oddities. How could we succeed at a *national* level? First, I identified our most likely customers: small to medium-size businesses. Second, I asked: What do they want to know? Of course, they wondered how to construct a web site. But that's what I wanted to sell them. They also wanted to know how to market their business on the Web, I reasoned.

So I scoured the rather sparse offering of articles on Web marketing available at that time, and began a link list of about 20 articles and resources. Then every month, without fail, I would scour the Web again looking for more materials. The Web Marketing Info Center (www.wilsonweb.com/webmarket) has grown into a resource containing links to 8,500+ articles and resources, the largest collection of information of its kind on the Web. In addition, I began to write articles explaining to small businesspeople how to market their site. Some of those articles were linked to by major sites and brought many visitors. We have become a Destination Site—on my more heady days, I like to consider us a Portal Site to the literature on Web marketing—and our business has prospered.

In mid-2001 the Internet is in a period of retrenchment. Free is out, fee is in. Battle-scarred survivors of the Internet slump react strongly to "free." The pendulum has swung too far in the fee direction. Web marketers need a balance of free and fee. Without free, your site loses a significant marketing advantage. Without fee, your site can't afford to stay in business.

Here's the simple strategy: (1) Attract people to your site by giving away lots of free information. Then (2) let people know about your products and services. Learn this rhythm of giving something away, and selling something. The strategy works. But to sell, you need to master a third law.

➤ 3. The Law of Trust

We talked about this in Chapter 15, "Building Trust in an Unknown Web Business." Assuming your products or services are priced competitively and are of good quality, your most significant sales barrier is trust. *Trust is the essential lubricant of Web business; without trust, business grinds to a halt.*

An established store brand name comes from hundreds of positive impressions built by expensive advertising campaigns. These ads purchase brand trust. But if you're a small business you can't afford such advertising. Nevertheless, you can build trust by means of your web site in multiple ways. First, anchor your business in time and space by giving a full address and phone number. If you have an office or brick-and-mortar store, show a photograph. Better yet, show photos of yourself or your staff. Now your customers view you as real people rather than some faceless entity who-knows-where.

You build trust by selling well-known brand name products, by displaying clear shipping and return policies, by joining nationally respected organizations, and by offering guarantees. You build trust with a customer-friendly navigation system and intuitive interface, and an SSL (secure sockets layer) server for credit card transactions. You gain credibility by having a professionally designed site, rather than something your teenage son cooked up on the weekends.

Once you've established trust, sales result. You also build trust by repeated contact with your visitors. We describe this in a fourth law.

➤ 4. The Law of Pull and Push

The Fourth Mutable Law of Web marketing is: *Pull people to your site by your attractive content, then push quality information to them regularly via e-mail.*

Web sites, by their very nature, are passive creatures, like fireside dogs. They just lie there wagging their tail listlessly and smiling wanly until someone enters the door. (Then the best web site dogs come alive and propel you to the desired destination and action.)

E-mail messages, on the other hand, are active animals like Saint Bernard rescue dogs, always ready to go where you send them, delivering a refreshing cask of information and an invitation to return to your web site to see the newest thing you have to offer.

A web site tries to attract you by *pulling* you in with the promise of content, while e-mail *pushes* its message into your previous visitors' mailboxes. Most businesses can't survive on one-time sales only. The cost of customer acquisition is too high for just a single sale. You need to draw satisfied customers back again and again for repeat sales. The Law of Pull and Push accomplishes this vital task.

Getting an invitation to send e-mail to your visitors is key to this strategy. Include a form that will collect their e-mail addresses. To convince your visitors to give you their e-mail addresses, however, you need to promise two things: (1) that you'll e-mail them something of value, and (2) that you won't sell or rent their addresses to another company, hence the need for a clear privacy policy. But once visitors have given you permission to e-mail additional information, you have wonderful marketing leverage.

How do you use it? If someone in your company has writing skills, you might develop a monthly newsletter. Beware. It takes real commitment and self-discipline to send out the newsletter regularly. But a regular newsletter will give a tremendous boost to your business, and will build your trust level with customers as well as bring them back to your site again and again. All of a sudden your company has top-of-mind position. Do this month after month and your brand recognition grows. If you're not a writer, you can send out monthly specials or news blurbs you garner (with permission) from other sites. Whatever you do, do it with excellence. Anything less than that will cause your business to lose the confidence you've already gained.

This law, too, has its own rhythm. Pull the customer to your web site by attractive power, then push good content and offers to the customer via e-mail to draw them back to your site.

➤ 5. The Law of the Niche

The Law of the Niche is last but not least. We already discussed this in Chapter 4, "Defining a Unique E-Business Niche." Let me state it this way: Big businesses like Amazon .com and Wal-Mart have the money and clout to "own" whole segments of the marketplace. *Small businesses succeed by finding niches that are either unfilled or only partially filled, and filling them with excellence.*

The Law of the Niche includes developing the Unique Selling Proposition that we discussed in Chapter 6. It is about hard work and differentiation and excellence, but this law isn't any more or less important than the other Immutable Laws of Web Marketing. They're all important. Together they offer you a path toward creating a successful business on the Web.

■ The Eight Essential Types of Internet Promotion

Sometimes your head can be so abuzz with Internet marketing details that you feel overwhelmed. You don't know where to start. You can't see the forest for the trees. While there is a lot of depth to be understood, I think that Internet promotion can be distilled down to eight essential types. Wrap your mind around these basic concepts and you can grasp what Internet promotion is all about. Here are the eight:

Search engines	Traditional media
Linking strategies	E-mail publishing
Viral strategies	Networking
Public relations	Paid advertising

Everything can be subsumed under these eight types of Internet marketing. If it's detail you want, read Appendix A, "The Internet Marketing Checklist: 27 Ways to Promote Your Website" or Susan Sweeney's book *101 Ways to Promote Your Web Site* (second edition, Maximum Press, 2000). But if it's simplicity you crave, I've tried to pare it down to the eight essentials.

➤ 1. Search Engines

Many people, perhaps even a majority of people, will use search engines and the Yahoo! directory to find what they're looking for on the Web. So the place to start in promotion is to design web pages that will be indexed well by the search engines, using descriptive titles and accurate META tags. When you're ready, submit your site so that search engines will index (spider) it, using a submission tool such as the All4One Submission Machine (www.all4one.com/all4submit) or JimTools (www.jimtools.com). Getting a listing in the Yahoo! directory is the most important task—and the most difficult. These days commercial sites have to pay Yahoo! $199 to consider within one week whether to add your site. Search engines are important. Be persistent. If your site doesn't show up within a few weeks, submit again . . . and again . . . and again.

But with hundreds of millions of web pages, and only 15% to 20% of them indexed, it's very easy for your site to get lost. The remedy (which adds to the clutter) is to create a set of doorway or gateway web pages, each tuned to score high on a specific search engine for a specific search word or phrase. While there is excellent software available for search engine positioning, Web Position Gold (www.webposition .com, $150), I recommend that small businesses outsource this task for $1,500 or so, plus a $100- to $150-per-month "mainte-nance" fee. The task is very time-intensive; it isn't really a spare-time project. There's more info in the Search Engine Marketing section of the Web Marketing Info Center (www .wilsonweb.com/cat/cat.cfm?page = 1&subcat = mp_Search).

➤ 2. Linking Strategies

Linking strategies are a second essential type of site promo-tion. The more links pointing to your site, the more traffic you'll experience (and the greater perceived popularity will rank you higher in the search engines). To get someone to link to your site you need to ask. The simplest way is to find complementary sites, link to them on a linking page, and ask them to link to you. The key, of course, is for your site to have content so good that it's worth linking to. No one wants to link to a nothing web site.

Ask for links on sites that cover your industry, as well as from associations your business belongs to. One twist on this is to join a Web Ring (www.webring.org) with each member site linking to the next member site along the chain. You might offer the best (and most trafficked) web sites an "award" that consists of an award logo with a link pointing back to your site. Another popular method is to join a banner exchange. For every two banners displayed on your site pro-moting other businesses, one of your banners will be shown on another member site. The biggest exchange is Microsoft bCentral LinkExchange (http://adnetwork.bcentral.com). Banner exchanges may help some, but don't count on a great deal of traffic here. I've given up on the so-called Free For All (FFA) linking sites; don't even waste your time there.

Another important form of linking promotion involves paying affiliates for sales resulting from links to your site, but we'll cover that under paid advertising.

➤ 3. Viral Strategies

An increasingly important process is to design a strategy that encourages others to carry your marketing message via e-mail, using their own network of relationships—and preferably their own resources. This is called "viral marketing" after the way viruses multiply rapidly in a cell, commandeering the cell's resources to do the virus's bidding. The classic example is HotMail.com, a free e-mail system. Each e-mail message (sent by definition to a person's own friends and associates) carries a message encouraging the recipient to sign up for a HotMail account, also. Another example is postcards or greeting cards, each of which carries a message encouraging the recipient to send a card to a friend—carrying the site owner's marketing message. If you can write quality articles, you can offer them to others to use on their web sites or in their newsletters, each article carrying a link to your web site. Public relations to get press coverage is a kind of viral strategy, if you think about it. More at the Viral Marketing Section of the Web Marketing Info Center (www .wilsonweb.com/cat/cat.cfm?page = 1&subcat = mm_Viral).

➤ 4. Public Relations

Public relations, the task of getting press coverage, is still a vital type of site promotion. If you can get a news release picked up by several print and/or Internet publications, you'll get a tremendous boost in traffic, all for "free," letting the news periodicals' network carry your marketing message. Of course, nothing's really free. You'll need to have a truly newsworthy event, contest, free service, chat room—or something—or no decent publication will consider it news. Coming up with "free" services and events isn't inexpensive, but the ensuing publicity can be excellent—you may get unbiased editorial recommendations that you couldn't purchase for any amount of money. While there are free news release services, expect to pay several hundred dollars to have your news release sent to hundreds of subscribing periodicals. More at the Public Relations Section of the Web Marketing Info Center (www.wilsonweb.com/cat/cat.cfm?page = 1&subcat = mp_PR).

➤ 5. Traditional Media

Don't discount traditional media in promoting your web site—news releases, of course, as well as paid advertising. A very effective way to promote your site is to place a small display ad in a targeted trade publication, offering some teaser copy and pointing readers to your URL or an autoresponder e-mail address for more information. This way your site serves as an online brochure, providing full information to interested shoppers day and night. A no-brainer is to make sure that all your company's literature, cards, letterheads, and envelopes carry your web site URL. If you're immersed in the Internet, you may have forgotten that most people still get the majority of their marketing messages through traditional channels. An excellent way for small businesses to learn how to use traditional advertising media is from Jay Conrad Levinson's *Guerrilla Marketing* (3rd edition, Houghton Mifflin, 1998).

➤ 6. E-Mail Publishing

If you're smart, you won't even think of developing a business web site without marrying it to an e-mail publication. The web site is the shy partner who passively waits for people to come to him. But the e-mail publication is the bold, active partner who goes out to where people are and invites them to come meet her groom. Together they make a great couple.

E-mail publishing is primarily a way to conserve the people who have shown some interest in your business by coming to your web site or responding to one of your offers. One of the highest priorities of your web site *must* be to get your visitor to sign up for your free newsletter, discussion list, or updates publication. Offer a variety of inducements—entry into a contest, a free gift, a free coupon—whatever you must do to insure a steady stream of subscribers to your newsletter. Once they are subscribers—if you give them content they enjoy and learn from—they'll stay with you for years, and you can gently build their trust month after month. When they're ready to make purchases, your site is at the top of their minds, and they'll probably buy from you. Figure the lifetime value to you of a single subscriber. When you've completed this exercise, you'll know why beginning your own e-mail publication is so vital to marketing your business. More info in the Newsletter and Discussion List Marketing Section of the Web Marketing Info Center (www.wilsonweb .com/cat/cat.cfm?page = 1&subcat = me_Newsletter).

Though some Internet marketers focus on sending stand-alone e-mail ads to their mailing lists, I shy away from that. With so much SPAM (unsolicited e-mail) abounding, it's too easy for recipients to mistake your promotion for just another ad, and unsubscribe forever. Though an occasional promotional e-mail may be okay, your marketing messages in the context of news and helpful information is much more effective and builds loyalty that you can never gain by just bombarding your customers with ads.

Of course, you probably know by now that sending out mass e-mails to huge lists of e-mail addresses is a no-no. It violates the principle of Permission Marketing that says people respond better to a marketing message they have agreed to receive. Unsolicited Commercial E-Mail (UCE) also runs contrary to a long-standing Internet tradition that responds to SPAM with angry flames and enough returned e-mail to cause your ISP to shut down your account very quickly. If you're interested in building a long-term business based on trust, don't send SPAM. On the other hand, a whole industry is developing, offering targeted opt-in e-mail lists for rent that we discuss below. See the E-Mail Marketing Section of the Web Marketing Info Center (www.wilsonweb.com/ cat/cat.cfm?page = 1&subcat = me_Email-Gen).

➤ 7. Networking

An extremely important way to promote your web site is through networking. Small business members of a local chamber of commerce know how making friends, being introduced, meeting new people at mixers, and being featured in the chamber newsletter can help build your business. Networking isn't quick, but it's the basis of relationships that will grow your business through word of mouth over the years.

On the Internet, networking is done primarily through newsgroups and e-mail discussion lists such as John Audette's venerable I-Sales Discussion List (www.audettemedia .com/i-sales). In discussion lists, people in an industry carry on a conversation about various current issues. After a while, you get to know the regular participants from reading their comments week after week. Regular participation fosters trust and builds your reputation. You don't brazenly hype your business in this kind of venue—that's considered rude. But the signature at the end of every e-mail message identifies you and tells people about your business and how to contact you. If you aren't using a signature in your e-mails, begin today. Search out the newsgroups and discussion lists in your industry and take an active part. This will result in increased traffic, as well as referrals and recommendations from list members to their other friends who might need your products or services. More info in the News Group and Mailing List Marketing Section of the Web Marketing Info Center (www.wilsonweb.com/cat/cat.cfm ?page = 1&subcat = mm_Newsgroups).

➤ 8. Paid Advertising

You'll notice that most of the first seven types of Internet Marketing can be done in-house relatively inexpensively (with the possible exception of search engine positioning). Of course, you may be able to find a marketing firm to which you can outsource some of these functions, but you can probably do a fine job yourself—after all, it's your business, and you are the one who can promote it most effectively.

But there comes a point when, to get wider exposure and break into the consciousness of the thousands of people who never haunt your end of the Web, you may need to resort to paid advertising. You'll be paying high-traffic sites or Internet publications to include a graphic or link that will channel large numbers of people to your site. There are several popular forms of paid advertising, with new approaches cropping up all the time.

Banner ads have been around the longest. Typically these are 468×60-pixel, animated, and linked graphic ads that appear at the top of a commercial web page. They are usually sold on a CPM (cost per thousand banner views) basis. Targeted sites may get CPM rates of $35 to $50 or more, but banner ads to reach general audiences are priced $1 to $10 CPM. Banners that pop up on search sites triggered by a keyword can cost $20 to $30 CPM.

But banner ads can be expensive. Do the math with me. If you're paying $10 CPM, and the click-through rate is 0.5%, then it costs you $10 to get 5 people to your site, or $2 each. If only 5% (or $1/20$th) of the visitors to your site make a purchase, then the "customer acquisition cost" is $2 × 20 or $40. You need a fairly high transaction total to pay out $40 per sale for customer acquisition. Your strategy, however, may be to pay a higher initial customer acquisition cost but get a customer you can keep and market to for the next several years. You may lose money on the first sale, but make it up on the second, third, fourth . . . and twentieth. More at the Banner Ads Section of the Web Marketing Info Center (www.wilsonweb .com/cat/cat.cfm?page = 1&subcat = ma_Banner).

Paid listings in portal sites. To get noticed, your online pet store may need to pay for a listing under the "Pets" category at Lycos Shop (http://shop.lycos.com). For this you may pay a flat fee or a percentage of the sale. Consider it the equivalent of paying rent to enjoy the foot traffic that a suburban mall might attract.

Sponsorships are longer-term paid ads on web sites or e-mail newsletters.

Pay-per-click links can be purchased on search engines such as GoTo.com (www.goto.com). The price per click for the top spots depends upon what you and your competitors are willing to bid. ValueClick offers banner advertising on a per-click basis (www.valueclick.com).

Pay-per-action advertising is popularly known as Affiliate or Associate Marketing. The merchant signs up a number of affiliates who place a link or linked graphic on their site. If a sale is made to a customer coming through that link, the affiliate earns a commission, typically 5% to 15% of the transaction total. This can be an effective—and safe—way to advertise, since you have to pay only when a sale is made. You can purchase software to run your own program, but I recommend outsourcing this to a service bureau such as Commission Junction (www.cj.com) that charges an initial set-up fee and then 20% of the commission you pay your affiliates. More info in the Affiliate Program Section of our E-Commerce Research Room (www.wilsonweb.com/cat/cat.cfm?page = 1&subcat = em_Associate).

Paid ads in targeted e-mail newsletters can be very effective. There are hundreds of thousands of e-mail newsletters, many of which have very modest advertising fees. Click-through rates are likely to be in the range of 1% to 3%. You'll find several e-zine directories in the Doctor Ebiz Directories of E-zines page (www.doctorebiz.com/01/000329c.htm).

Opt-in e-mail advertising involves sending a stand-alone ad for your business to individuals who have (hopefully) volunteered to receive information from your kind of business. These are called "opt-in" lists, since the list members have agreed to receive information. Avoid "opt-out" lists where recipients are placed on a list involuntarily and then invited to unsubscribe if they want to. Opt-in lists can be quite targeted, with ads getting a 1% to 3% click-through rate. Expect to pay 10¢ to 25¢ per name; the list broker will do the e-mailing on your behalf. You'll find a list of brokers in the Targeted Direct E-Mail Lists Section of the Web Marketing Info Center (www.wilsonweb.com/webmarket/lists.htm).

Certainly, there are many more types of paid advertising, but these are some of the most common and most effective.

Internet promotion can seem overwhelming. But hopefully it's more understandable since we've outlined the eight types that comprise effective web site promotion. Here they are, once again:

Search engines	Traditional media
Linking strategies	E-mail publishing
Viral strategies	Networking
Public relations	Paid advertising

. . .

Exercise: List the major Internet promotion strategies you will use to promote your site. Then try to estimate the parameters and price of each approach you select.

■ Developing an Effective Internet Promotional Mix

Here's the number one question I am asked: "How can I get more traffic to my web site?"

Here's the consultant's answer—and the truthful answer: "It all depends."

➤ What Your Web Site Tells Your Visitors

First of all, until your web site is in good shape, you can spend a lot of money bringing traffic to your site, but you won't do much business. Have you ever seen a store on a street in your town where the owner decided he could skip paying a professional sign maker and paint the sign himself? When he's finished, he's really impressed with what he has been able to accomplish with his limited experience. He brings his wife over.

"Great sign, right, dear?"

"Remarkable, Henry," she comments.

He shows it to his brother-in-law and to his best friend. And he's so excited about it that they don't want to burst his bubble by telling him the truth: "Henry, it may be a real accomplishment for you, but it looks cheap and homemade. It won't grow your business. In fact, it will deter customers from coming into your store."

Ad agencies have complained to me that companies are spending tens of thousands of dollars in advertising, but their web sites turn people off when the advertising succeeds in getting them to the site. One of the first steps in your site promotion strategy is to get your web site ready to sell effectively. It'll never be perfect, it'll always be a work in progress, but it needs to look very good.

➤ What's Next?

All of the "Eight Essential Types of Internet Promotion" are important. You can't neglect search engines or public relations or any of the others. But very high on your list needs to be developing a regular e-mail publication and an effective way to get your visitors to subscribe when they visit your site. We're too small, you say? Nearly all e-mail publications start small. But you have to begin. Don't put it off, for it becomes more and more powerful later as your list begins to grow.

➤ Mud on the Wall

I'll tell you a secret. What works splendidly for Marketing Guru A, works only so-so for Marketing Guru B. The reason is that companies are different, budgets vary, the ability to innovate changes in different contexts. Yes, you can learn from marketing gurus, but don't be surprised if their pet programs don't quite produce the same results in your corner of the world.

You've probably realized by now that I believe in planning and working out careful Web marketing strategies. Yes, but I also know that you'll never learn what works best until you try a lot of things that show some promise. There's an old saying, "If you throw enough mud against a wall, some of it is going to stick." Hmmm . . . strange saying. But it's true. Try a number of things, see what works best for you, and then focus more of your resources on the things that work. Don't be afraid to try new things, and don't be afraid to fail. But don't make long-term investments in strategies you haven't first experimented with on your site.

For example, let's say your company sets the annual Internet promotion budget at $400 . . . or $4,000 or $40,000 or $400,000—it doesn't matter. If you're just beginning, I recommend making short-term contracts where possible, so you can try out various approaches, but still have the flexibility to shift significant funds to the approaches that work.

Don't be afraid of failure. Your role in the company is to learn everything you can, including the things that don't work. If one method bombs, don't quit. Keep at it until you find a mix of methods that are effective for you.

■ Outsourcing Web Site Promotion

Smaller companies will probably need to outsource some of the site promotion functions. Here are some guidelines and kinds of companies to look for.

In the United States there are many good companies to which you can outsource promotional campaigns. In other countries these services are still developing.

But you must realize that it's not wise to outsource the function of marketing director to some outside firm. You, or someone in your own company, must understand and direct your marketing efforts. Yes, bring in a consultant to help you strategize, but you must internalize, understand, and own the strategies in-house. Then you can outsource certain functions to others.

I'm often asked to recommend companies that provide web site promotional services. Nearly all have specialties; few will hold your hand and lead you to web site success. A few companies that cater to small to medium businesses offer a broad variety of Internet marketing strategies and services. One of the best is Webster Group International (www.wgi.com) in St. Louis, Missouri. But finding success is ultimately your responsibility. A marketing company may execute a program for you, but *you* must decide whether this program will be a wise one to accomplish your overall Internet Marketing Plan.

Following are the types of companies I find available. I'm listing just a few examples of each, but there are many, many excellent companies. Use the appropriate Yahoo! Directory listing to find others in each category. One general category is "Marketing and Advertising | Internet | Promotion."

Search engine registration services. Remember, don't pay much here, since perhaps only 10 search engines plus Yahoo! are likely to bring you much traffic anyway. Example: Microsoft bCentral SubmitIt (submitit.bcentral.com). You can do this yourself with free services such as All4One Submission Machine (www.all4one.com/all4submit) and JimTools.com (www.jimtools.com).

Search engine positioning services help raise your ranking on the search engines. Plan on paying $1,000 to $4,000 upfront, and $100 to $500 and up per month. Examples: CoastalSites.com, Web-Ignite.com, and iProspect.com. Yahoo! category: "Search Engine Placement Improvement."

Ad agencies help you place your ads on targeted sites and newsletters where they will do the most good. There is no charge to you, but the ad agency makes its money by paying 15% less on ads they place with a web site. You may need a monthly advertising budget of $5,000 or so before an ad agency will take you on. Examples: Beyond Interactive iFrontier.com. Yahoo!: "Marketing and Advertising | Internet | Advertising."

Banner ad graphic artists help you design a creative banner ad. Examples: LoungeLizard.com, BannerWorkz.com, and GWWebDesign.com.

Banner ad networks place ads for you on their own network of sites. Some, like DoubleClick and FlyCast, provide very sophisticated services for larger clients. Other networks include Microsoft bCentral LinkExchange. Yahoo!: "Internet | Promotion | Banner Exchanges."

Copywriters help you write compelling ad copy for e-mail marketing. Found under many categories.

E-zine ad agencies help place ads for you in targeted newsletters within their networks. See List-Advertising.com's directory (www.list-advertising.com/ad-networks).

Press release services send your news releases to hundreds or thousands of online and offline news media. Examples: XpressPress.com and Internet News Bureau. Yahoo!: "News Services | Press Releases."

Public relations services help your company develop ongoing press coverage in online and offline media and handle relations with the press. Yahoo!: "Corporate Services | Public Relations."

E-mail opt-in list brokers will find appropriate e-mail lists that meet your marketing objectives. They handle the outgoing e-mail and often provide response tracking, among other services. Example: PostMasterDirect.com. See the Lists page in the Web Marketing Info Center (www.wilsonweb.com/webmarket/lists.htm).

Affiliate programs allow you to pay for ads or links only when they result in a sale. Examples: Commission Junction, BeFree, LinkShare, and My Affiliate Program. See the Affiliate Program Section of the E-Commerce Research Room (www.wilsonweb.com/cat/cat.cfm?page = 1&subcat = em_Associate).

Chapter

20

P4—Price: Pricing Strategy

Every site on the Web has a pricing strategy, but most are guesses, not deliberate marketing choices. And most will lead to business failure. Here's how to develop your own clear pricing strategy.

When you go down to your local grocery store, you'll probably find Jif® peanut butter, and maybe Planter's®, and then perhaps a store brand. For some product categories the store brand products are actually manufactured by the name brand companies. Yet each has a different price, and each product has a different price strategy. These are marketing decisions, pure and simple. The 4 Ps of Marketing are elements of the marketing mix that you can control. Price is one of the key elements in a winning marketing mix.

You can't do business on the Internet without having a pricing strategy. And though it may seem pretty simple on the surface, your company's pricing strategy can easily mean the difference between thriving and going bankrupt. A lot of factors are involved.

One of the first questions you need to answer is: What are

your site visitors like? Are they bargain hunters? Do they look for excellence in customer service? Or shop for products based on their prestige value? Another important question is: What does it cost you to purchase (or produce) and market this product or service? Your price will have to be above your costs—most of the time. Here are the various pricing objectives you'll want to consider.

■ Pricing Objectives

Two main pricing objectives stand out:

To maximize short-term profits. Here you try to squeeze as much money out of sales of the product as possible, even though fewer customers may make a purchase. Your strategy may be to charge premium prices for web site design services. Or you may need to maximize profits in order to satisfy an impatient boss or investor. You end up with fewer customers, but then dealing with a lot of customers multiplies your problems. And you can make more profit from each customer.

To gain market share. The other main strategy is to price your service lower to gain market share. You may want to maximize the number of subscribers to your online Internet access business, even though you don't make as much on each customer. But you know that later you'll be able to sell these subscribers other services such as Web hosting, e-commerce, web site design, DSL, and a host of others once they get comfortable with you. You don't make as much early on, but you plan to make money later with back-end sales.

These two objectives are the key ones to understand, though two others may also figure in:

To survive. Survival is a worthy goal. Sometimes companies lower prices so they can generate enough revenue to survive short-term. But this isn't a very good long-term strategy. There's an old joke about the businessman who said he was losing money on every sale, but he expected to make it up in volume. Good luck. Sometimes it's better to call it quits before you lose even more.

To help society. You might keep the price lower than "what the market will bear" in order to make essential products available to the consumers who would otherwise be priced out of the market. Altruism has its place. You don't have to make as much money as possible, unless making money is your only goal. For example, I really want to keep my consulting services priced within reach of small businesses. I long to see small businesses thrive; that's part of what makes me tick. But I also want to charge better-funded companies a more appropriate fee for the more extensive services I render to them. The way I do this is to offer a standard product or service, and an economy service at a lower price, but with clear limitations.

There's no way in the scope of an article this size to go into all the factors involving setting a price for products or services. You'll find whole books written about this subject, for example, *Strategy and Tactics of Pricing: A Guide to Profitable Decision Making,* by Thomas T. Nagle and Reed K. Holden (second edition, Prentice Hall, 1994). Others are available for particular industries, crafts, and services.

■ Customer Demand

Consumer demand is a crucial factor. Demand is driven by consumer tastes, consumer income, and the availability of other products at a different price. For example, if a competitor begins to sell 6-oz. Styrofoam cups at a lower price than yours, the demand for yours will decrease. Professional pricing consultants construct demand curves to determine absolute demand. Newsweek conducted a study wherein it sold its magazine at a variety of lower newsstand price levels in different U.S. cities. They learned just how much lowering the price in 50-cent increments would increase the total copies sold by plotting sales figures on a demand curve. They even calculated demand if they were to give the magazine away. (1) Direct marketers test different "offers," different ad copy, and different prices by using "split lists," sending different offers to different parts of the list. There are ways to do this with web pages, too. Marty Foley's Victory Ventures now offers the Scientific Web Marketing System that allows Web marketers to do split-run testing by showing different web pages to different visitors (http://profitinfo.com/yoap/bin/deliver.cgi?swms-1492).

Of course, commodities, well-known products that are pretty much the same as every other similar product, are strongly affected by demand as well as supply. Take crude oil, for example. If it's abundant, prices drop. If it's in short supply, though, and customer demand remains constant, the price goes up. You could always sell beans or corn or pork bellies on your web site. But the price would be constantly changing. You need a great product that you have more control over. Producing your own product, or getting exclusive marketing rights, of course, is best if you can do it.

But having a great and exclusive product is only half the battle. Making the customer aware of its existence and its value is the other, and that's the role of marketing. You can increase demand by advertising and careful pricing.

■ Estimating Revenue

Once you've established consumer demand, you need to estimate revenue. It helps to master a few technical terms:

Total revenue is the unit price multiplied by the quantity sold.

Average revenue is the average price the product sold for. This is still pretty simple. Now buckle your seat belts.

Price elasticity of demand is another concept. Think how much stretch a rubber band has in it. "Elastic demand" is when a small decrease in the price of Styrofoam cups produces a big increase in sales. "Inelastic demand" is when a small decrease in the price of cups makes only a tiny difference in sales.

Fixed cost comprises the fairly stable overhead costs of running the company, such as lease on the building, management salaries, insurance, and a Picasso print on the wall of your office.

Variable cost is the direct cost of production and marketing. This will vary with the number of goods produced and sold, such as labor and materials used in manufacturing. It costs you more for widget makers and widget glue when you produce more widgets.

Total cost is the sum of the fixed cost and the variable cost.

Break-even analysis is pretty straightforward. You determine the level of sales needed to cover the total costs and break even. Any sales after that start to accrue profits.

Determining that maximum profit point is a vital goal in pricing. This takes some research and then some mathematical analysis and graphing. I'm pretty excited about a new web-based tool, **Make Your Price Sell!** (http://sales.sitesell .com/myps), that promises to make this research and price calculation relatively fast and easy. Without the kind of scientific study this tool enables, price setting—of an e-book, for example—is pretty much a matter of guesswork. With this kind of tool, pricing of products and services can be determined so you can maximize sales or maximize profits, whichever you choose. (See my review later in this chapter.)

■ Pricing Approaches

Of course, pricing isn't just scientific. It has a lot to do with your particular niche on the Internet and how you've determined you can best succeed. Here are some demand-oriented approaches to pricing.

Skimming pricing. When you are offering a new or innovative product, you can initially charge a high price, since the "early adopters" aren't very price-sensitive. Then you lower prices to skim off the next layer of buyers. Eventually, the price will drop as the product matures and competitors offer lower prices.

Penetration pricing. You set a low initial price in order to penetrate quickly into the mass market. A low initial price discourages competitors from entering the market, and is the best approach when many segments of the market are price-sensitive. Amazon.com, for example, offers a discount price and may lose money on the first sale, but this way they gain more customers who will purchase products later at a lower marketing cost (since it costs much less to attract them back for the second or third sale if they are happy with their first purchase experience).

Prestige pricing. Cheap products are not taken seriously by some buyers unless they are priced at a particular level. For example, you can sometimes find clothing of the same quality brand at Nordstrom as you do at the Men's Warehouse. But because it is priced higher, Nordstrom's clientele believes it to be of higher quality.

Odd-even pricing takes advantage of human psychology whereby $499.95 feels like much less than $500. Studies of price points by direct marketers have found that products sell best at certain price points, such as $197, $297, or $397, compared to other prices slightly higher or lower. Strange, we humans!

Demand-backward pricing is sometimes used by manufacturers. First, they determine the price consumers are willing to pay for a product using an approach such as Make Your Price Sell! automates. Then they work backward through the standard markups taken by retailers and wholesalers to come up with the price they can charge wholesalers for the product.

Bundle pricing is offering two or more products together in a single-package price. This can offer savings to both the buyer and to the seller, who saves the cost of marketing both products separately. And customers are willing to pay more because they perceive that they are getting a lot more, even though the cost to the seller may not really be that much greater.

Here are some cost-oriented approaches to pricing that I'm sure you are familiar with:

Standard mark-up pricing. Typically a manufacturer marks his price up 15% over his costs, a wholesaler 20% over his costs, and a retailer 40% over his costs. The retailer gets a larger markup based on the idea that, since he is closest to the end user, he is required to spend more services and individual attention meeting the buyer's needs.

Cost-plus pricing prices by adding a small percentage to the retailer's costs—and "cost plus 5%" sounds so modest in ads for new cars! Ah! If only it were that simple.

Experience curve pricing assumes that it costs a company less to produce a product or provide a service over time, since learning will make them more efficient.

Then there are competition-oriented approaches to pricing that you'll recognize:

Customary pricing is where the product traditionally sells for a certain price. Candy bars of a certain weight all cost a predictable amount—unless you purchase them in an airport shop.

Above-, at-, or below-market pricing. Certain stores advertise low-cost or discount pricing. Others price at the market, while others deliberately price above the market at premium prices to attract prestige buyers.

Loss-leader pricing works on the basis of losing money on certain very low-priced advertised products to get customers in the door to buy other products at the same time.

Flexible-price policies offer the same product to customers at different negotiated prices. Cars, for example, are typically sold at negotiated prices. Many B2B sales depend on negotiated contracts.

Once you have determined the list or quoted price, you can make some special adjustments still:

Quantity discounts encourage customers to buy larger quantities, thus cutting marketing costs for the merchant.

Seasonal discounts encourage buyers to stock inventory earlier than their normal demand would require. This enables the manufacturer to smooth out manufacturing peaks and troughs for more efficient production.

Rebates, such as $40 off a software program, are usually offered by the manufacturer, but sometimes a retail store will offer its own rebate. Rebates make marketing sense, since they strongly motivate sales, but often less than 50% of the buyers will remember to collect the receipt, proof-of-purchase, and rebate form, fill it out, and mail it prior to the expiration date. And, of course, the rebate is often subtracted from the list price of the item, which still has considerable profit built in. Rebate marketing is less than half as expensive to the marketer as the price cut would seem to indicate.

Trade discounts are offered by manufacturers to distributors or resellers in their distribution chain. For example, a manufacturer may quote a list price of $1,000 less 30/10/5, meaning 30% off the list price to the retailer, an additional 10% off the $1,000 to the wholesaler, and an additional 5% off the $1,000 to the jobber. This pricing will be expected if you have an online B2B store.

Cash discounts are sometimes offered for the costs saved by not having to extend credit and bill the buyer on an open account. This mainly affects B2B sales rather than retail.

Allowances may be permitted for trade-ins (not too many trade-in cars are shipped by modem, though) or by a manufacturer for promotional advertising that a retailer undertakes.

Geographic adjustments involve FOB (Freight On Board) pricing at the point of shipping. Shipping costs are added when an item is listed FOB.

■ Regulations on Pricing

Finally, we need to note that there are various governmental regulations on pricing. If you sell outside your own country (and having a global marketplace is the beauty of the Internet!), you need to familiarize yourself with laws in other countries.

In the United States, for example, conspiring with other firms to set prices for a product is called price-fixing and is illegal. Price discrimination—different prices to different buyers of the same goods or services—is tricky. The U.S. Robinson-Patman Act allows for price differentials only under certain circumstances. Deceptive pricing is outlawed in the U.S. by the Federal Trade Commission. Predatory pricing, that is, charging a very low price with the purpose of driving competitors out of business, is illegal in the United

States under the Sherman Act and the Federal Trade Commission Act, but is hard to prove.

I've just scratched the surface of pricing. Left unexplored are price-raising strategies, product line strategies, marginal analysis, and much more. But this will give you enough to get your imagination going.

■ The Take-Away Lesson

What's the take-away lesson from all this? You need to think through and then adopt a very deliberate price strategy. Look at the examples in the next section. Will you sell what are essentially commodities and be the low-price leader? Or the service leader? Will you deliberately price low in order to penetrate the market quickly and establish first-mover advantage? Or will you price high to skim off the early adopters at a premium profit? Will you bundle several products in order to make a greater profit? Will you round off to the nearest dollar or use an odd-price approach? Do you have a new or exclusive product that you can study scientifically for the best price?

Most online businesses only guess at prices—and most will be out of business in a few years as a direct result. The best online businesses are very deliberate about pricing, do their homework, and make changes quickly when necessary. Do your very best with pricing. After all, pricing is the only one of the 4 Ps of Marketing that brings revenue in rather than sending it out.

Exercise: Carefully study the pricing strategy that fits your business and your niche on the Internet. Then write the rationale for your pricing strategy in a single short paragraph.

■ Decision: Web Examples of Deliberate Pricing Strategies

With some of this background under your belt, let's look at some examples of these strategies and approaches on the Internet.

➤ Commodity Pricing

If you're a retailer, will you be the low-price leader? That's tough to do unless you have some pretty good purchasing strategies that allow you to compete with bigger companies. Sales of computer hardware and software don't leave much of a margin for profit. *PC Magazine* awarded Microsoft Front-Page 2000 their Editor's Choice designation. ComputerShopper.com found 19 merchants that carried it. Table 20.1 provides a few of these prices as of 5/8/00. Each store has a well-thought-through pricing strategy—or it won't be in business very long.

Table 20.1　Low-price Leader Pricing Strategies

	Price	Compared to buy.com
CompSource	$146.26	+19.9%
CDW	$135.40	+11.0%
PCStop.com	$131.56	+7.9%
MicroWarehouse	$129.95	+6.5%
Page Computer	$129.28	+6.0%
Dell	$127.95	+4.9%
PC Zone	$124.97	+2.5%
Amazon.com	$121.99	—
buy.com	$121.95	—
PC Mall	$121.89	—
PCWonders.com	$118.89	−2.5%

Buy.com has a price strategy of rock-bottom cost plus very little, supplemented by banner advertising revenue. Will this pricing strategy allow them to stay in business? Only time will tell.

Dell is nearly 5% over buy.com, and leverages its huge buying power. I've bought products from CDW (11% over buy.com) and MicroWarehouse (6.5% over buy.com) and been pleased with their service. I've also bought from buy.com, Dell, and Page Computer with good results.

Most small businesses will die in this environment of razor-thin margins. A better spot is to find a niche in the shadows of the bigger players.

► Penetration Price Strategy

Ken Evoy's first product, an e-book entitled *Make Your Site Sell!* (http://sales.sitesell.com/myss), is a good example of a penetration strategy. His e-book on maximizing sales using direct marketing techniques on the Web was priced at $24.95 Canadian (U.S. $17), substantially below many other marketing courses. His goal was to grow a loyal team of well-paid affiliates to help him market a whole series of products. So he deliberately priced *MYSS!* relatively low in order to get as many sales—and quality affiliates—as possible. Now with a list of many thousands of very satisfied customers, he is beginning to launch several new products.

Make Your Knowledge Sell! (http://sales.sitesell.com/ myks) is a comprehensive how-to book on creating, developing, marketing, and distributing information products such as e-books, cassette tapes, and so on. The pricing for this product was scientifically determined through surveys completed by Evoy's army of affiliates. Though it has fewer pages than *MYSS!*, the price is higher: $79 Canadian, and just over U.S. $50. But he has determined what his customers perceive it to be worth, and it is selling very well—partly because it delivers on its promise as the "Infopreneur's ToolKit." This certainly isn't the aggressive penetration strategy of *MYSS!*, but knowing Ken, I expect it's priced below the maximum profit point.

Make Your Price Sell! (http://sales.sitesell.com/myps) is Ken's latest product, a service that enables marketers to scientifically determine the best price for their products. He developed and used it to price *MYKS!* and is now turning it into a product in its own right. The price? In order to achieve strong penetration into the market, Ken is allowing users to pay what they think it's worth to them—at least for the first few months.

Ken's strategy is not short-term gain, but long-term profits. He is carefully developing a loyal customer base that appreciates the value he brings. The initial product price may be U.S. $17, but the lifetime value of these customers is many, many times that.

➤ Maximum Profit Price Strategy

Here's an information product with a different strategy. Cory Rudl's *Insider Secrets to Marketing Your Business on the Internet* (www.marketingtips.com/t.cgi/15267) is priced at $197, an important price point. It costs about 11 times as much as Ken Evoy's *Make Your Site Sell!*, probably contains a similar number of words, and is arguably no better for its higher price. Rudl's greatest strength in this very practical book is how to do e-mail marketing, a subject that Evoy comments on only in passing. They are very different approaches to Internet marketing, and both very helpful. Is Rudl's course worth $197? In my somewhat critical review (www.wilsonweb.com/reviews/rudl-secrets.htm) of the product, I conclude that it is. Certainly Rudl has a different pricing strategy than Evoy, probably a maximum profit approach. He also sells the following two software programs at premium prices that marketers can make excellent use of.

Mailloop Business Automation Software (www .marketingtips.com/mailloop/t.x/15267) is a desktop program that helps marketers send out and track mailings to their customer lists, as well as manage newsletter lists. There's nothing quite like it in this price range, but at $379 you probably wouldn't think of it as a "bargain," rather as an expensive tool that enables you to move your marketing to the next level. Pricing strategy is behind this.

AssocTRAC Affiliate Software (www.marketingtips.com/ assoctrac/t.x/15267) isn't inexpensive either. But at $677, the tool allows you to track, and therefore maximize the effect of, all your site's advertising and offers. Instead of just tracking click-throughs, the product allows you to relate a particular ad to sales directly generated by that ad and determine return on investment for every ad on every site that you place. Not cheap, but an effective pricing strategy.

You'll notice the difference between the pricing of Microsoft FrontPage 2000 and the proprietary products sold by Evoy and Rudl. While FrontPage 2000 is sold by thousands of dealers for various prices, Evoy and Rudl have exclusive control of their products and services. This enables them to set their own prices based on customer demand rather than reaction to pricing by competitors.

As you study prices on the Internet, you'll find many examples to learn from. But don't take forever to learn. Use these lessons to set your own deliberate pricing strategy as part of your Internet Marketing Plan.

■ Review: *Make Your Price Sell!*

Make Your Price Sell!
http://sales.sitesell.com/myps
by Ken Evoy and Carol Ann Dorn

Goodbytes Information Products Inc.

Priced around U.S. $20

I'm thinking about producing some information products to sell on the Web. But how should I price them? I wonder. I can look at something similar and price them like that. Nightingale-Conant Corp. (www.nightingale.com) sells self-help information products. Then I look at something at my local Borders bookstore and wonder if I'm pricing too high. What is the right price? What is the best price for my information products? Now I know how to find the answer.

I'm very excited about Ken Evoy's new Make Your Price Sell! online service. The system consists of an online survey you can customize and cut and paste into your web site. After describing your product or service as clearly and compellingly as you are able, you have your customers fill out a short survey. The answers are recorded and analyzed in the MYPS! server and offer you powerful insights into how to price your products.

➤ Six Key Questions

The survey consists of three pairs of questions that deal with:

Product impact. How unique and important your respondent considers it.

Net buying habits. How often your respondent buys this type of product and how much he or she usually spends.

Price points. What your respondent considers a "fair" price for the product and where the "Teeter Point" is.

The "Teeter Point" is a key piece of information (and Evoy has trademarked the term). Half your respondents are asked, "What price is almost too high to buy this product?" The other half are asked, "What price is just a bit too high to buy this product?" In other words, where is the point that respondents really have to struggle to decide whether they should buy the product or not?

➤ Graphs

The beauty of MYPS! is in the graphs it produces. The "How important is the product to you?" question results in a bar graph (Figure 20.1). The "How much do you usually spend for this kind of product?" question shows another bar graph (Figure 20.2). The "What is a fair price for this product?" question graph shows a scattering of answers from low to high. But the graph enables you to see the clustering (Figure 20.3). The real genius of Make Your Price Sell!, however, is found in the composite graph (Figure 20.4).

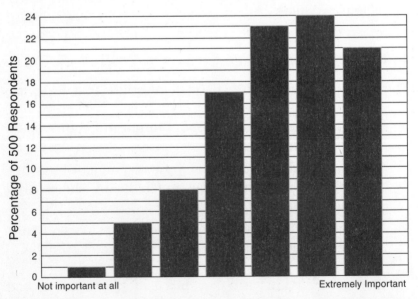

Figure 20.1   How important is the product to you? (Copyright © 2000–2001, SiteSell.com, used by permission. All rights reserved.)

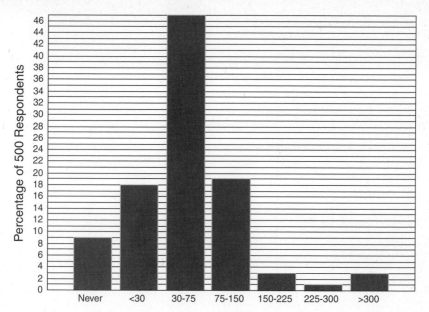

Figure 20.2   How much do you usually spend on this product?
(Copyright © 2000–2001, SiteSell.com, used by permission. All
rights reserved.)

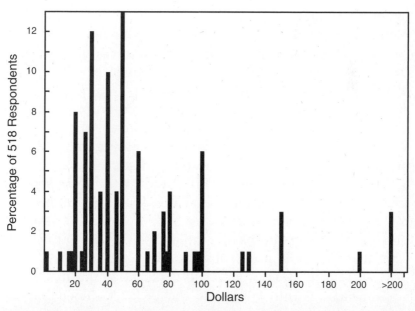

Figure 20.3   What is a fair price for this product? (Copyright © 2000–
2001, SiteSell.com, used by permission. All rights reserved.)

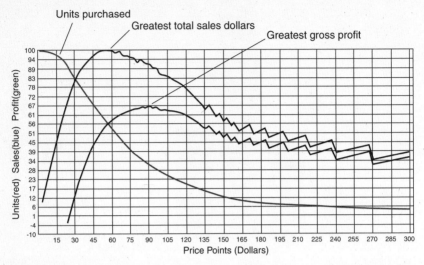

Figure 20.4 Composite graph. (Copyright © 2000–2001, SiteSell.com, used by permission. All rights reserved.)

It takes a bit of work to understand the composite graph, but it is an effort very much worth the time. The program plots smoothed data obtained from respondents into single curves. In the example shown in the manual, one line displays the drop-off in units purchased as the price increases. A second line looks like a dome with its top arching over right at $57, which is the price point at which the program has determined you will make your greatest total sales dollars— that is, you will sell the product to the greatest number of people. The third line is a shallower dome that peaks right about $90, the price point at which you will make the greatest gross profit. You sell fewer products at this higher price, but the higher margin means you make a higher profit. After $90 the maximum profit point passes, though slowly. The graph indicates that you could price substantially higher than $90 for a price-skimming strategy, and still make a tidy profit.

So where should you price the product shown in this example? If you have a penetration price strategy, the price should be around $57. For a high-profit strategy you would price around $90. Your final price depends upon the pricing strategy you've set as part of your overall Marketing Plan.

The 122-page manual provides a lucid explanation of pricing theory, and then describes exactly how to use MYPS! to determine price. It includes twelve ways marketers can find the right people to fill out the online survey, and it notes that price consultants may want to administer the survey in paper form and later input the answers into the MYPS! online interface. Considering the quality of information the graphs offer, this will expand the toolset of many consultants.

➤ Weaknesses

Make Your Price Sell! isn't perfect. The graph indicating price peaks (Figure 20.4) shows jagged stair-step "peaks" off to the right side of the graph. The uninitiated might mistake them for meaningful price points, while in actuality they are graphing artifacts resulting from sparse data on that edge of the graph. The plotting program should have smoothed them out. The text interpreting the graph can be improved, too, explaining the price points the graph is showing you. I would have liked the ability to isolate the responses of those who were the most frequent purchasers of the product type, since this would tell me what those who actually purchased such products thought of them, rather than diluting their insights with the opinions of respondents who didn't purchase this type of product very often. MYPS! offers a way to look at the answers of your best prospects, but doesn't really explain how this is determined. Like any first generation software product, MYPS! has a few rough edges that will need to be smoothed and features that need to be expanded in later versions.

➤ The Bottom Line

MYPS! succeeds wonderfully at its chief goal: to provide marketers with a scientific tool that will help them set their product's perfect price. And for the first time it makes available to mere mortals on the Web the sophisticated analytical tools to which only high-priced consultants were once privy.

➤ Reference

1. Cara S. Trager, "Right Price Reflects a Magazine's Health Goals," *Advertising Age,* March 9, 1987, pp. 5–8ff. Cited in Berkowitz, et al., *Marketing* (fifth edition, Irwin, 1997), pp. 375, 377.

Chapter

21

Budgeting for and Implementing Your Internet Marketing Plan

We've spent a long time on planning. Now it's time to connect money and action to your plan in order to propel your e-business to success.

■ How Much to Budget for Marketing

One of the most obvious questions after doing all the planning is: How much money do you need to budget for marketing? I've heard a couple of rules of thumb.

Spend as much on start-up marketing as you did to build your web site. Good, but incomplete. This rule has the advantage of being flexible, since the amount spent on web sites varies from a few hundred dollars to millions of dollars. The point of this rule is that setting up a web site isn't enough—your marketing has just begun.

Spend 20% of your gross revenues on sales and marketing expenses. Good, but only for a maintenance budget of an e-business that has been up and going for a while. A company (or Internet branch of a company) in the start-up mode should expect to spend a lot more on marketing—even 50% the first year. Getting your online presence known and beginning to attract online customers can be quite expensive.

■ Determining an Online Widget Marketing Budget

The best way to determine how much you need to spend for marketing is to determine your sales objectives and then work backward, using some educated guesses. For example, let's say that your initial objective is to sell 1,400 widgets from your web site over the next twelve months. How big a marketing budget will that require? To get a handle on costs we need to estimate two rates, the web site conversion rate and the advertising response rate.

➤ Web Site Conversion Rate

The conversion rate (CR) is the percentage of web site visitors who actually make a purchase. This typically varies from 0.5% to 5% depending upon a number of factors. A good estimate, if you have no track record to guide you, is 1%. But this 1% can be driven up dramatically as you learn to fine-tune your site to propel the sale more effectively.

➤ Advertising Response Rate

The response rate is the percentage of ad impressions or exposures that elicit a response. For online media this response is usually termed the Click-Through Rate (CTR). Let me give you some ballpark rates for various kinds of online media.

The average CTR for banner ads shown to a general audience is usually under 0.5%, or 5 clicks per thousand impressions. This goes up when the site is more targeted or when the banner ad is shown in response to a search word. You might get 1% to 2% on a more targeted site, and perhaps 5% to 10% widget prospects will click on a widget-focused banner that is displayed when someone types in the search word "widget" on a search engine.

Text ads in e-mail newsletters will bring about a 1% CTR, perhaps more. A stand-alone e-mail ad, sent out to a targeted opt-in e-mail list, might bring a 1% to 3% CTR.

Of course, all these CTRs are subject to wide variation. I've seen banner ads targeted to my web site clientele that consistently bring a 5% to 10% CTR. An ad written with a compelling headline and powerful, motivating copy could increase the CTR for e-zines and opt-in lists to 5% and more. But be conservative for your initial budget estimates. You'd rather have your boss happily surprised than yourself humiliated when your ad campaign bombs after an all-too-rosy budget projection.

➤ Calculating the Number of Impressions Needed

Here's the formula to calculate the number of impressions needed:

$$\text{Ad Impressions Needed} = \frac{\text{Units to Be Sold}}{(\text{CR} * \text{CTR})}$$

Let's assume that a 1% Conversion Rate (CR) and a 0.5% Click-Through Rate (CTR) are appropriate for our widgets, and we need to sell 1,400 widgets online over twelve months. Here's how you determine the number of advertising impressions you'll need:

$$\text{Ad Impressions Needed} = \frac{1,400}{.01 * .005}$$
$$= 28,000,000$$

➤ Calculating the Cost to Sell 1,400 Widgets

Once you know the number of impressions you need to sell your goal of 1,400 widgets, you can begin to set a budget.

It is possible to purchase banner ads for $3 per 1,000 impressions, or $3 CPM (Cost Per Thousand). At $3 CPM, you can purchase 28 million untargeted impressions for $84,000. Next, determine the advertising cost per unit sold.

$$\text{Advertising Cost per Unit} = \text{Advertising Costs/Units Sold}$$
$$= \$84,000/1,400$$
$$= \$60$$

If your widgets sell for $495 each, then $60 is an appropriate advertising cost. But if your widgets sell for $29.95, then you'd better refigure your ad budget dramatically to reduce costs.

➤ Ways to Decrease Advertising Cost per Unit

When you look at the formulas used to calculate advertising cost per unit, only three elements are variable—CTR, CR, and CPM. Therefore, to decrease the ad cost per unit we need to either raise the Click-Through Rate and/or the Conversion Rate, or reduce the Cost Per Thousand of advertising impressions.

Raising the click-through rate (CTR). You can do this by improving your banner ad creative, writing a more effective text ad, or finding more targeted locations in which to place your ad. Doubling the conversion rate from 0.5% to 1%, for example, can cut in half your advertising costs.

Raising the conversion rate (CR). The conversion rate on a new web site can usually be improved dramatically. Single-product sites would do well to study the techniques found in Ken Evoy's *Make Your Site Sell!* (http://sales.sitesell .com/myss). For online stores with multiple products I've written *12 Ways to Give Your Webstore a Sales Boost* (www .wilsonweb.com/ebooks/sales-boost.htm). Doubling the conversion rate from 1% to 2% can cut your advertising costs by half, also.

Lowering the cost per thousand (CPM). You're not going to find paid advertising much below $3 CPM, but if you could find advertising for $1 CPM, wouldn't that do wonders for your budget? Many ads now are purchased on a Cost Per Click (CPC) or Cost Per Action (CPA) basis, so you pay only when someone responds or makes an actual purchase. Another approach is to look at other traffic-driving methods besides paid advertising, such as search engine optimization, news releases, reciprocal links, and e-mail ads sent to your own house e-mail list.

The central challenge of preparing an Internet Marketing Budget is determining how to spread your available dollars in order to achieve your sales objectives. Let's examine how to do that.

■ What to Include in Your Budget

Let's distinguish first between your Marketing Department Budget and the money you'll need to budget to accomplish your Marketing Plan. Generally, your Marketing Department Budget will include salaries and other employer costs for each of your employees. There will also be items to cover fixed overhead costs.

Your Marketing Plan Budget, on the other hand, consists of the direct costs for various marketing activities, not including department salaries. The Marketing Plan Budget is traditionally divided into three main categories.

Advertising. The cost of preparing the art and writing copy (creatives) for your advertising, as well as the cost of purchasing advertising (media buys).

Publicity. This covers the cost of representing your company to the public through news releases and various kinds of public events.

Promotion. Promotion includes such items as the 5% discount you're planning to offer in your Fall Campaign, as well as mouse pads bearing your company logo and pens with your company name.

■ Three Sample Internet Marketing Budgets

To give you an idea of how this might work, let's look at three imaginary companies promoting their e-business—medium, small, and very small. Perhaps you can see your company in one of these. Realize, however, that the marketing mix selected for each of these companies is not prescriptive for your company, but rather suggestive. You'll need to determine for yourself what works for your company. There is no cookie-cutter formula, so these budgets are designed to help you in the beginning stages of developing a budget for your Internet Marketing Plan.

➤ Huntington West Surfboards Online

Huntington West has been online for three and a half years, with a full e-commerce function for the past two years. While Huntington West has been selling surfboards and surfing supplies through sales reps to retail stores and through catalogs for years, the Internet Marketing Budget includes only the marketing of the Internet sales arm. Average monthly online sales is about 20 surfboards, plus accessories, averaging $784 plus shipping and tax per transaction (Table 21.1).

Table 21.1 Huntington West Annual Advertising Costs

Type of Advertising	Specifics	Annual Site Visitors Generated	Annual Cost
Banner ads	SurfsUpHawaii.com, $2 CPM, 50K per month, 2% CTR	12K	$1,200
Banner ads	ActiveSportsNuts.com, $5 CPM, 100K per month, 1.25% CTR	15K	$6,000
Search engine keyword banners	Average cost of $30 CPM and 12% CTR. About 14,000 click-throughs per year for the words "surf," "surfboard," "Woody," and "hang 10"	14K	$3,500
Banner ad creatives	Designs a minimum of 12 new banner ads per year, with a goal of 5 ads achieving a 2% CTR on targeted sites	–	$2,400
Search engine optimization	Paid for initial optimization last year. Now pays monthly maintenance fee. Optimized for "surf," "surfboard," "surfer," and 13 other words.	205K	$1,800
Display ad	1/8-page display ad 6 times per year in *Ride the Wave* magazine	8K	$6,000
	Advertising Totals	**254K**	**$20,900**
Publicity			
News releases	Four news releases per year to coincide with interest in major surfing exhibitions; cost of distribution through three major online news release channels	42K	$3,000
Trade show	Shared space with traditional marketing branch; 3 shows per year, 30% of space	4K	$2,250
Trade show fliers	Color fliers for distribution at trade shows and surfing exhibitions	20K	$4,000
	Publicity Totals	**66K**	**$9,250**
Promotion			
5% summer sale	Costs 5% off net price of surfboards sold in May	–	$784
$50 rebate	$50 rebate, with a 40% return rate on rebate coupons	–	$4,800
	Promotion Totals	–	**$5,584**
	Marketing Plan Totals	**320K**	**$35,734**

Table 21.2   TheFriendlyFrogs.com Annual Advertising Costs

Type of Advertising	Specifics	Annual Site Visitors Generated	Annual Cost
¹/₁₆-page display ad	*Reptilian Times*, each issue published six times a year	12K	$2,700
¹/₁₆-page display ad	*Amphibian Lovers Quarterly* published four times a year	11K	$1,800
Search engine optimization	Initial charge plus 6 months of maintenance for gateway pages tuned for the words "amphibian," "frog," "newt," and "salamander"	36K	$2,100
E-zine sponsorship	WetWay Collectors e-mail newsletter, published monthly; sponsorship, $50/month.	24K	$600
	Advertising Total	**83K**	**$7,200**
Publicity			
	News release prior to the Reptile and Amphibian convention	15K	$225
	Publicity Total	**15K**	**$225**
Promotion			
	"Feed Your Frog" flyswatters bearing TheFriendlyFrogs.com logo and URL for distribution at the convention	3K	$250
	Promotion Total	**3K**	**$250**
	Marketing Plan Total	**101K**	**$7,675**

➤ TheFriendlyFrogs.com

TheFriendlyFrogs.com (Table 21.2) is a small amphibian site, which provides supplies and specimens exclusively for amphibian collectors. Jack Green runs the operation out of his home, and drop-ships through three equipment suppliers, except for the live specimens that he grows in one of his bedrooms. (His wife and daughters moved out when the girls were forced to share a bedroom so his frogs could have one of their own.) His sales last year were about $50,000.

➤ ClownAroundVideo.com

George Clowny is just starting up his online business to sell video tapes of clown skits to people learning to be clowns.

Table 21.3 ClownAroundVideo.com Annual Advertising Costs (projected)

Type of Advertising	Specifics	Annual Site Visitors Generated (hoped for)	Annual Cost
Classified ad	Classified ad in ClownTownDown monthly magazine, $50 per month	3K	$600
Search engine positioning	Purchase of WebPosition Gold software; George plans to do his own search engine positioning and invest the time necessary	70K	$150
	Advertising Total		**$750**
Publicity			
	News release related to the popularity of clowning in the U.S.; distributed through free press release web sites		
	Publicity Total		**$0**
Promotion			
	Promotion Total		**$0**
	Marketing Plan Total	83K	$750

Most of the expense of making the video tapes was covered by a friend who had the equipment and did the editing at no charge. But George can't afford much at all for his Internet Marketing Budget, since he doesn't know yet how well his tapes will sell (Table 21.3).

■ Implementation Plan

Part of any Internet Marketing Plan, even for a single-person business, needs to be an Implementation Plan. This is essentially a calendar of activities, with dates, person responsible, and cost. Without a schedule and persons taking responsibility, all the planning is in vain. Here's an example of the month of May for Huntington West Surfboards Online (Table 21.4).

Table 21.4 Implementation Plan for Huntington West

Date	Action	Cost	Person Responsible
4/1	Check CTRs for banner ads run in April. Consider changes if rate has dropped significantly.		Ron
4/5	Set up the May 5%-off sale. Prepare copy for ads to be placed on web site. Check to see that creatives are on track to be sent for advertising to begin May 1.		Erica
4/7	Analyze traffic logs to determine traffic from search words. Analyze monthly positioning report from positioning firm.		Ron
4/10	Prepare news release to coincide with May 5%-off sale and surfing exhibition.	$2,500	Erica
4/15	Distribute news release.		Erica
4/25	Rewrite copy for color fliers to be distributed at summer trade shows and surfing exhibitions.		Erica

Once you prepare it, your implementation guide will keep you on track even when you're discouraged. The marketing you do, month in and month out, will have an effect.

Exercise: Prepare an Internet Marketing Budget and an Implementation Plan for your site for the next 12 months.

Part V

Putting It All Together

Up to now we've looked in detail at the various stages of planning marketing for your online business. It can seem pretty overwhelming, but in the final chapter I want to explain just how you can write a formal Internet Marketing Plan that you can use to raise capital from external sources, or to enable internal readers to understand and implement the company's Internet strategies.

Chapter 22

Writing Your Internet Marketing Plan

If you are required to write out your Internet Marketing Plan, here is a format and some guidelines for each section.

Many readers will be expected to write out a formal Marketing Plan for their company. But even if this isn't a requirement, the discipline of writing down what you've learned about your company forces you to think through each strength and weakness, each opportunity and problem, and devise strategies to meet each. Even if you have a small mom-and-pop business, you'll find great value in writing out your plan—though you won't have to work so hard to impress the "boss." It helps insure your survival. This is what a Marketing Plan does for you:

An Internet marketing plan forces you to think through your strategy carefully and *spot holes* in your business concept that you'd otherwise miss.

The process of researching and writing forces you to think and plan—and careful *planning* is one of the keys to success.

Then, too, when you've written your marketing plan, even an abbreviated plan, you can share it with your Certified Public Accountant or a Small Business Administration advisor to get *feedback*. The more critiquing your Internet Marketing Plan receives prior to execution, the better the Plan will be.

An Internet Marketing Plan helps you *keep on track*. Since you'll know your break-even points, you'll be able to better judge where you are, and be motivated to meet stated objectives and milestones.

Finally, an Internet Marketing Plan forces you to *assess your competitors,* and on the Internet there are many more than in any single geographical area. A competitive analysis helps you to differentiate your business and thus increase its chances to stand out and attract new customers.

■ Separate or Integrated Marketing Plans?

Some companies will have only an e-business focus, but an increasing number of companies have both traditional and e-business aspects. Should you have separate Marketing Plans for your Internet and traditional channels?

Only you can answer that question. I'm in favor of integrating the plans, so far as you are able, since there will be a lot of overlap. On the other hand, a company's Internet offering may be only a slice of its traditional menu of goods and services. Competitive factors may be vastly different; so will marketing strategies. Perhaps you can get away with the Internet Marketing Plan as part of the overall Marketing Plan, using shared sections where possible.

■ Differences between a Business Plan and Marketing Plan

What's the difference between a Marketing Plan and a Business Plan? The Marketing Plan may comprise 60% to 70% of the entire Business Plan, depending upon the type of business. However, a Business Plan contains additional details on research and development, operations, and manufacturing activities. Often there is a section on financing arrangements that wouldn't be part of a straight Marketing Plan.

■ Focus on the Reader

As you prepare to write your Marketing Plan, consider your readers, your target audience. Is this an internal audience who will implement the plan? Is it an external audience, with banks, venture capitalists, and potential investors? If so, then it must also be a sales document, and will be more detailed, especially in financial information, than an internal Marketing Plan. Seek to answer your audience's questions. Here are some common questions that *external* audiences have in their minds:

- Is the marketing idea valid?
- What differentiates the products, service, or company from competitors?
- Is there a clear market?
- Are financial projections realistic and healthy?
- Are key personnel experienced and capable of accomplishing the Plan?

- Does the Plan indicate how investors will get their money back and make a profit?

An *internal* audience may not be so critical, but they will be the ones who, by their everyday conversations and meetings, represent the company's products, plans, and unique offerings to customers and the press. Hopefully, the Plan will both inspire and motivate them with its boldness, its promise, and the rational presentation of its projections for the company's future.

■ Writing and Style

As in all good business writing, the style should be clear and direct. If your goal is to convince others of the validity of your Plan, be positive without resorting to hype. Since this may be a relatively long document, use plenty of headings and subheadings to make it more readable. Bullet points convey the essence without taking much space. The final report can be printed by ink-jet or laser printer, and collated copies bound inexpensively at a local copy shop.

■ Overview of the Marketing Plan

To lower your level of anxiety about this Marketing Plan, there is no single right way to put together a plan, no single outline you must follow. Even the experts don't always agree. In this chapter we'll recommend a particular approach that has logical consistency, but if a different order of presentation works better for your company, go for it. Don't let the formality intimidate you.

Here's a basic structure for your written Marketing Plan. A realistic goal might be to write 15 to 30 pages, not counting your financial projections. But if you can communicate the important elements clearly in fewer words, don't just fill out space.

Table of Contents

Executive Summary

Company Description

Strategic Focus and Plan

Situation Analysis

Product Focus and Positioning

Marketing Program Strategies

Financial Data and Projections

Organization

Implementation Plan

Evaluation and Control

Appendixes

➤ Table of Contents

Your Internet Marketing Plan will begin with a cover page (displaying your company logo, perhaps) and then a table of contents so your readers can quickly grasp where you are going, and how the Plan is structured.

Section 1. Executive Summary

Why is it that executives have a summary just for them? Are they stupid? No, just busy. If you can't outline the case for your Internet Marketing Plan in a page or two, why should an executive read through the whole boring document? In a sense, the executive summary sells the rest of the Plan.

The executive summary is probably the best read and therefore most important part of your Plan. It rests, however, on all the research and study required to write the Plan itself. I encourage you to write the executive summary last, after you've written everything else. These are the pages to write and rewrite, for they set the tone for everything else. Set yourself a limit of about two pages, or 500 words.

Section 2. Company Description

For an internal audience or perhaps a new start-up you might be able to skip this section. But if your Plan's readers may include outsiders, here you write a few paragraphs about the company's background, general position in the market, and recent successes. Your goal is to convince readers that the company has direction and momentum. Try to limit yourself to four paragraphs.

Section 3. Strategic Focus and Plan

This section will have three main sections: (1) a succinct statement of your mission or vision, (2) goals for the coming year (or five years), and (3) how your company's core competencies translate into a sustainable competitive advantage.

3.1. MISSION OR VISION   Here's where the work you've done to develop a Unique Selling Proposition (USP, Chapter 6) becomes part of your plan. Write this USP in a format that mentions your company's major stakeholders—customers, employees, and stockholders.

For example, here is a USP: "FrogLover.com is your destination shop for amphibians: supplies, books, information, research, and gossip—the most comprehensive amphibian site on the Web."

Your mission or vision, then, is "To provide the most comprehensive amphibian site on the Web, with supplies, books, information, research, and gossip provided in such a way that customers find excellent value for their money, employees are challenged and rewarded, and shareholders receive above-average returns." One or two sentences are all that is necessary.

3.2. GOALS FOR THE COMING YEAR(S) In Chapter 7 we talked about setting strategic goals for the organization—both financial and nonfinancial goals. In the Marketing Plan you'll want to list these goals, since many of them directly relate to the marketing function of the organization. The best goals are not just platitudes, but clear, time-bounded, measurable statements about the future that can be checked later to see if they have been accomplished or not. This isn't the place to spell out tactics or methods, but for overall goals and objectives for the organization. Expect to take one or two pages. Later in the Plan you'll spell out more clearly the specific marketing goals that support your organizational goals.

3.3. CORE COMPETENCY AND COMPETITIVE ADVANTAGE In Chapter 5 you began to assess your company's core competencies. Value derives directly from the competencies that you possess and develop. And your competitive advantage is sustained only to the extent that you use and develop these core competencies wisely. State briefly what you perceive your competencies to be, and how this affects your competitive advantage. This is not the place for hype, but for an accurate assessment of the value your company brings to the marketplace. A paragraph or two ought to be enough.

Section 4. Situation Analysis

Much of your research has gone into analyzing the marketing situation. Here is where you discuss your core findings. If you have detailed studies that are important, but not quite central, why not include those in an appendix to the Internet Marketing Plan? The Situation Analysis section is the place for summary tables, graphs, and charts that distill your research. This section includes: (1) SWOT analysis, (2) industry analysis, (3) competitive analysis, (4) company analysis, and (5) customer analysis.

4.1. SWOT ANALYSIS The familiar four-quadrant table we used in Chapter 8 summarizes strengths, weaknesses, opportunities, and threats. No need to present the SWOT analysis in the table, but discuss briefly each of the four elements, each in a single paragraph. If one of these sections is the basis of major assumptions that your Plan is based on, feel free to develop it into a two- or three-paragraph treatment, but no more. Brevity and crisp analysis are the goal here.

4.2. INDUSTRY ANALYSIS The industry analysis we discussed in Chapter 9 outlines current trends in the particular industry and niche your company is serving. In this section indicate that you understand current trends and directions, and that your marketing strategies are designed to work with these trends, rather than at cross-purposes to them. This builds confidence in your readers that your company understands the industry thoroughly. However, do not mistake understanding for a multitude of words. Try to sketch the trends and your related strategies in two or three paragraphs. You can show supporting graphs and charts in the text or, even better, in an appendix.

4.3. COMPETITIVE ANALYSIS Your careful study of a unique e-business niche in Chapter 4 and your studies of competitors in Chapter 10 form the basis of this section. If you have external readers, they'll want to be sure that you've selected a business niche in which you can succeed vis-à-vis your competition. Name your major competitors and their market share, their strengths and their weaknesses. If you have no real competition, explain why this is so. Make sure you discuss the barriers to competition that prevent your competitors from taking over your unique e-business niche. This section should take a page or two, depending upon the degree of competition in your niche. Support your analysis with charts and graphs, either here or in an appendix.

4.4. COMPANY ANALYSIS Logically, the Company Analysis directly follows the Competitive Analysis to explain how your company is well fitted to meet the competitive challenges. If you are writing to an external audience, this is part of your sales piece. Plan on a page or so. If your primary audience is internal, don't spend time preaching to the choir; summarize in a paragraph or so and move on.

4.5. CUSTOMER ANALYSIS Another key piece of research that underlies your marketing strategy is the customer analysis that you conducted in relation to Chapter 11. You'll probably want to include customer surveys and demographic analyses in an appendix, with the results distilled in words and graphs in the body of the Marketing Plan. You'll want to cover customer characteristics, customer trends, and a calculation of your Customer Lifetime Value, which will drive your marketing financial analysis. The Customer Analysis may require two or three pages, since a clear customer focus is the key to your business success.

Section 5. Product Focus and Positioning

New companies often offer a single product or service. But as companies mature they build on their strengths and respond to competitive opportunities they see in the marketplace. This section deals with the company's plans to extend new product lines into new market areas. It may involve the rollout of new products or services. This section will typically have four subsections: (1) marketing and product objectives, (2) target markets, (3) points of difference, and (4) positioning.

5.1. Marketing and Product Objectives This section will detail how products and services will be delivered to current markets and new markets, and how products and services will be adapted and extended into new offerings. Drawing on your research in the Situation Analysis section, you'll be stating measurable and time-bounded marketing objectives that both take advantage of the gaps you have discerned and build on your company's strengths. These objectives undergird the strategic organizational goals mentioned in Section 3.2 above. If the objectives in Sections 3.2 and 5.1 overlap too much, consider combining both in the same section at this point in the Plan. Depending upon the maturity and complexity of your company's product and service line, this section might involve a page or two.

5.2. Target Markets Based on your studies of prospective customers in Chapter 11 and segmenting your Internet market in Chapter 12, now you describe clearly your company's target market(s). This is best if concise, so try to sketch your target market in a couple of sentences, no more than two paragraphs.

5.3. Points of Difference Drawing upon your Situation Analysis in Chapters 8 through 11, as well as exercises in Chapter 13, you'll spell out the points of difference that make your products and services unique relative to your competitors. If you're a new Internet company, this may involve differentiating your company itself from the competition. Spell this out clearly, since this information is vital to helping your internal readers develop sales and marketing approaches, as well as convincing your external readers of your company's future. Without differentiation, your company cannot succeed. Make this section crisp and short, just a paragraph or two to make these distinctions, or a series of bullet points.

5.4. POSITIONING Points of difference between your company and the competition show the differences. The step to positioning is a small but important one, and relates to your company as a brand, which we discussed in Chapters 13, 14, 15, and 16. In a sentence or two spell out how precisely you wish to position your company, products, and services in your customers' minds. This is a very brief but crucial part of your Marketing Plan as you develop advertising copy to project your positioning to the marketplace.

Section 6. Marketing Program Strategies

Use the classic 4 Ps to flesh out your marketing program: P1. Product Strategy, P2. Place (Distribution) Strategy, P3. Promotion Strategy, and P4. Price Strategy.

P1. PRODUCT STRATEGY Product strategy, as you discovered in Chapter 17, includes the line and quality of products or services you offer, but also relates to the packaging of your web site—a rationale for its look and feel. Depending upon how complex your line of products and services, this P1 might require one to three pages.

P2. PLACE (DISTRIBUTION) STRATEGY As Chapter 18 indicates, the way products and services are delivered as a result of Internet sales usually involves a deliberate choice of drop-shipping, inventory, fulfillment house, and downloading, or a combination of these. If you are a manufacturer this requires a decision if you'll sell directly to the end user and bypass the traditional distribution chain. It also includes shipping strategies. You'll need to spell out your choice of a distribution strategy, and how this choice will leverage important advantages, and how you'll deal with the methods' inherent disadvantages. Two or three paragraphs will probably suffice.

P3. PROMOTION STRATEGY Promotion is what many novice Internet businesspeople envision when they think of marketing. As you have seen, marketing planning involves a whole spectrum of decisions that must be made. If these decisions have been made correctly, then promotional strategies can help the company succeed. But if the marketing planning is flawed, even lots of money spent on promotion won't salvage the company. List the types of promotion you plan to employ here. You may select promotion methods from a list in Appendix A, The Internet Marketing Checklist. The budget you plan to allocate to each method is spelled out in Section 7, and the Implementation Schedule is detailed in Section 9. Subsection P3 will probably take two or three paragraphs to perhaps two pages. If you have external readers especially, you'll probably want to include a rationale of why each method is essential to accomplishing your overall marketing objectives.

P4. PRICE STRATEGY As you learned in Chapter 20, pricing strategy is part of the picture of positioning your company as the low-price, or quality, leader. State your price strategy succinctly. You'll probably need just a paragraph or two.

Section 7. Financial Data and Projections

We haven't treated financial projections in this book, so you may need to draw on the help of your accountant or chief financial officer for this. You have a twofold task: to project sales revenues expected from your strategies and implementation schedule (as we glanced at briefly in Chapter 3) and to demonstrate a growth in the operating profit from one quarter to another. It is here in the financial section that external Marketing Plan readers will be spending much time and analysis.

The longer an operating history your company has, the easier it is to make accurate projections. If you are making assumptions—and all plans make a number of assumptions—be sure to clarify in writing each assumption that affects your financial projections. Don't hide your assumptions, since the validity of your assumptions is key to the Plan's validity and your company's success. If outside eyes can help you develop more realistic assumptions, they are doing you a big favor in the long run.

Even if your Marketing Plan is intended for internal readers, the time you spend making quarterly revenue and net profit loss projections is time well spent. You may decide, as I have on occasion, that certain pet projects may be successful and well received, but aren't worth pursuing from a financial perspective.

There is no way to predict the length of this section. If possible, place your conclusions in the text to keep the logical argument flowing, and put supporting tables and documents in the Appendixes.

Section 8. Organization

Whether or not you include an organization section depends upon your Marketing Plan's purpose and readers. While internal readers may be interested in seeing an organizational chart, external readers need to be convinced that your company's team of executives and other personnel have the experience and credentials to make the company succeed. You may want to include photos and short biographies of key personnel here, with full resumes in an Appendix. For some internal Internet Marketing Plans this section can be eliminated altogether.

Section 9. Implementation Plan

The Implementation Plan often takes the shape of a Marketing Calendar, and details exactly which methodologies need to be implemented on which date to accomplish the Plan's objectives. If you have a small company, it is useful for internal readers that this section be quite detailed, with dates, tasks, and persons responsible for each task. External readers will be more interested in the overall strokes. A Five-Year Plan will sketch out only the outlines of an implementation plan to show how different strategies will phase in at different times. Let your needs dictate the length of this section.

Section 10. Evaluation and Control

The final section of the written Marketing Plan will detail how performance will be evaluated, and the marketing program modified, depending upon results. This can be a very general statement, or more detailed as needed. Probably a paragraph or two is sufficient.

Appendixes

The Marketing Plan's appendixes will provide supporting material for the conclusions reached in the text body. Don't just include materials to pad the report, but those items that may be of interest to those examining your methods, assumptions, calculations, and conclusions.

Appendix

The Internet Marketing Checklist: 27 Ways to Promote Your Web Site

We've included an appendix to provide additional materials and examples for preparing your Internet Marketing Plan.

You have a web site, but it isn't getting the number of visitors you'd like. What can you do to stimulate traffic? Why don't you take a few minutes to review? Here's a checklist of 27 items you need to consider. Many of these you're probably doing already; others you meant to do and forgot about; still others you've never heard of. Of course, a great deal has been written about this. You'll find links to thousands of articles on site promotion in our Web Marketing Info Center (www .wilsonweb.com/webmarket). While we're not breaking any new ground here, we've tried to summarize some of the most important techniques.

The most important first step is to register your site with the main Web search engines, so we begin with steps to prepare your Web pages for optimal indexing. We link to lots of info on search engines at www.wilsonweb.com/cat/ cat.cfm?page = 1&subcat = mp_Search.

1. *Write a page title.* Write a descriptive title of 5 to 8 words for each page. Remove as many filler words as you can from the title, such as "the," and "and." This page title appears on the Web search engines when your page is found. Entice surfers to click on the title by making it a bit provocative. Place this at the top of the Web page between the ⟨HEADER⟩⟨/HEADER⟩ tags, in this format: ⟨TITLE⟩Web Marketing Checklist -- 27 Ways to Promote Your Site⟨/TITLE⟩. Hint: Use some descriptive keywords along with your business name on your home page. Instead of "Acme Cutlery, Inc." use "Acme Cutlery--Pocketknives, Butchering Sets, and Kitchen Knives". The more people see in the blue highlighted portion of the search engine that interests them, the more likely they are to click on the link.

2. *List keywords.* To get your juices flowing, sit down with some associates and brainstorm a list of 50 to 100 keywords or key phrases—the kind of words or phrases someone might use to search for a business or site like yours. Then refine the list to the most important 20 or so. Place those words at the top of the Web page, between the ⟨HEADER⟩⟨/HEADER⟩ tags, in a META tag in this format: ⟨META NAME="KEYWORDS" CONTENT="promoting promotion Web marketing online sales . . ."⟩

   Note, however, that some research on search engine algorithms indicates that a fewer number of keywords may help you better target the most important search words if you're working to increase your page's ranking on the search engines. Consider using both lowercase and capitalized forms of your very most important words, since some search engines are capitalization-specific. Make sure that you don't repeat any word more than three times so you're not penalized for keyword spamming.

3. *Write a page description.* Select the most important 20 keywords, and write a careful 200- to 250-character (including spaces) sentence or two. You don't need to repeat any words used in the page title. Keep this readable but tight. Eliminate as many filler or throwaway words as you can (such as: and, the, a, an, company, etc.) to make room for the important words, the keywords which do the actual work for you. Place those words at the top of the Web page, between the ⟨HEADER⟩ ⟨/HEADER⟩ tags, in a META tag in this format: ⟨META NAME="DESCRIPTION" CONTENT="Increase visitor hits, attract traffic through submitting URLs, META tags, news releases, banner ads, and reciprocal links"⟩.

4. *Submit page to search engines.* Next, submit your page to the important Web search engines and directories. To do this, consider using a submission service such as www.JimTools.com or All4one Submission Machine (www.all4one.com/all4submit). The most important search engines that robotically spider or index your site are AltaVista, Google, Excite, HotBot, Lycos, Infoseek, WebCrawler, and Northern Light.

5. *Submit page to Yahoo!* Yahoo! is the most important listing of all—though it's technically a directory, rather than a search engine. It uses real humans to read (and, too often, pare down) your 200-character sentence, so be very careful and follow their instructions (www .yahoo.com/docs/info/include.html). Hint: I've learned to use less than the maximum number of characters allowable. If the Yahoo! editor starts chopping your wordy copy, he or she may not leave as much as you'd like. In mid-2000 Yahoo! instituted a $199 fee for businesses that want their listings to be considered for the Yahoo! directory. It's worth it, since Yahoo! can bring a great deal of traffic.

6. *Submit page to other directories.* You've probably seen offers to submit your pages to 300 different search engines. These don't help much, except to increase the perceived popularity of your site by some of the major search engines. The most important 25 directories are probably enough, unless you find some specific to your industry. Most of the rest aren't really search engines at all, just an excuse to solicit you for upgraded listings. These marginal directories come and go very quickly, making it hard to keep up.

7. *Include URL on stationery, cards, and literature.* Make sure that all reprints of cards, stationery, brochures, and literature contain your company's URL. And see that your printer gets the URL syntax correct. In print, I recommend leaving off the http:// part and including only the www.domain.com portion.

8. *Promote using traditional media.* Don't discontinue the print advertising you've found effective. But be sure to include your URL in any display or classified ads you purchase in trade journals, newspapers, and the like. View your web site as an information adjunct to the ad. Catch readers' attention with the ad, and then refer them to a Web page where they can obtain more information or perhaps place an order. Sometimes these ads are more targeted, more effective, and less expensive than online advertising. Consider other traditional media to drive people to your site, such as direct mail, classifieds, and postcards. Since Super Bowl 1999 we've seen TV used extensively to promote sites, because the Web is now considered a mass medium, though it is probably too broad for all but the most general products and sites.

9. *Develop a free service.* It's one thing to say, "Come to our site and learn about our business." It's quite another to

say, "Use the free kitchen remodeling calculator available exclusively on our site."

Make no mistake, it's expensive in time and energy to develop free resources such as our Web Marketing Info Center (www.wilsonweb.com/webmarket), but it is very rewarding in increased traffic to your site. Make sure that your free service is closely related to what you are selling so the visitors you attract will be good prospects for your business. Give visitors multiple opportunities and links to cross over to the sales part of your site.

10. *Request reciprocal links.* Find complementary web sites and request a reciprocal link to your site (especially to your free service, if you offer one). Develop an out-of-the way page where you place links to other sites so you don't send people out the back door as fast as you bring them in the front door.

11. *Request links on industry sites.* You probably belong to various trade associations that feature member sites. Ask for a link. Even if you have to pay for a link, it may bring you the kind of targeted traffic you crave.

12. *Request links from business link sites.* Especially if you offer a free service, you can request links from many of the small business linking pages on the Web. When you have something free to offer, many doors open to you. Surf the Net looking for places that might link to your site. Then e-mail the site owner or webmaster with your site name, URL, and a brief, 200-word description of what you offer there.

13. *Issue news releases.* Find newsworthy events (such as launching your free service), and send news releases to print and Web periodicals in your industry. Note: Opening or redesigning a web site is seldom newsworthy these days. You may want to use a Web news release

service, such as one offered by Eric Ward's URL wire (www.urlwire.com) or Internet.com's Internet News Bureau (www.newsbureau.com).

14. *Capture visitor e-mail addresses and request permission to send updates.* On your web site's response form, include a check-box where the visitor can give you permission to e-mail updates about products or services. Now your e-mails to visitors are not considered spam. You're responding to their request for more information. I recommend capturing first and last name in separate fields so you can market personally to them. But ask only for the information you need or they won't fill it out.

15. *Publish an e-mail newsletter.* While it's a big commitment in time, publishing a weekly, monthly, or quarterly newsletter is one of the very best ways to keep in touch with your prospects, generate trust, develop brand awareness, and build future business. You can distribute your newsletter using your e-mail program, or have people subscribe on your web site directly to a listserver. More information can be found at www .wilsonweb.com/articles/newsletter.htm. Why don't you take a look at our newsletter, *Web Marketing Today* (www.wilsonweb.com/wmt), and subscribe free, like tens of thousands of others?

16. *Install a signature in your e-mail program.* Most e-mail programs such as Eudora, Netscape, or Outlook allow you to designate a signature to appear at the end of each message you send. Limit it to 6 to 8 lines: company name, address, phone number, URL, e-mail address, and a one-phrase description of your unique business offerings. Look for examples on e-mail messages sent to you.

17. *Promote your site in mailing lists and newsgroups.* The Internet offers thousands of very targeted mailing lists

and newsgroups made up of people with very special-
ized interests. Use Google Groups (http://groups.google
.com) to find appropriate sources. Don't bother with
newsgroups consisting of pure spam. Instead, find
groups where a dialog is taking place. Don't use aggressive marketing and overtly plug your product or service, even if you see someone doing so. Rather, add to
the discussion in a helpful way and let the signature at
the end of your e-mail message do your marketing for
you. People will gradually get to know and trust you,
visit your site, and do business with you.

18. *Join a mall.* You may gain a little traffic this way, but not
a lot. The biggest and freest mall, if you will, is Yahoo!
Get a good listing there, and you won't need other malls
very much. Paying to be in a mall is seldom a good
investment, though Web stores may want to pay for vis-
ibility on a major portal site.

19. *Announce an incentive or contest.* People like getting
something free. If you publicize a contest or drawing
available on your site, you'll generate more traffic than
normal.

20. *Join a banner exchange program.* Of the many banner
exchange programs, LinkExchange is the biggest (www
.linkexchange.com). Essentially, you agree to show a
rotating banner on your site for other LinkExchange
members, and they do the same for you. A full list
of banner exchange programs can be found at www
.bannertips.com/exchangenetworks.shtml.

21. *Purchase banner ads on appropriate sites.* You may need
to spend money to boost traffic by purchasing banner
advertising. Choose sites that seem to attract the kinds
of people who would be good prospects for your business or product. Expect to pay $3 to $20 per thousand
people who see your ad, and achieve a click-through

rate of 0.5%. You can find media brokers who can help you find appropriate and cost-effective places to advertise, especially if you have a significant advertising budget for branding purposes. Much information exists at www.wilsonweb.com/cat/cat.cfm?page = 1&subcat = ma_Banner.

22. *Buy a text ad in an e-mail newsletter.* Businesses are finding that some of the best advertising buys are for small 4- to 8-line ads in established e-mail newsletters. Ads can both inform and motivate readers to click on the URL, and tend to bring much more targeted visitors. There's more info at www.wilsonweb.com/cat/cat.cfm ?page = 1&subcat = me_Email-Gen.

23. *Rent targeted, opt-in e-mail lists.* We abhor spam, bulk, untargeted, unsolicited e-mail, and you'll pay a very stiff price in reputation and cancelled services if you yield to temptation here. But the direct marketing industry has developed targeted e-mail lists you can rent consisting of people who have agreed to receive commercial e-mail messages. Do a smaller test first to determine the quality of the list. Some companies which offer such services are listed at www.wilsonweb .com/webmarket/lists.htm.

24. *Employ search engine positioning.* Registering your site with the search engines is the first step. But with tens of millions of web pages, your site may hardly be visible. These days you may need to construct a series of gateway pages, each tuned for a particular search phrase and search engine. Then fine-tune these gateway pages to rank high, using a program such as Web Position Gold (www.webposition.com). Many small businesses outsource search engine positioning because of the considerable time investment it requires. You can

find more information at www.wilsonweb.com/wmt4/
issue54.htm.

25. *Begin an affiliate program.* Essentially, a retailer's affiliate
program pays a commission to other sites whose links to
the retailer result in an actual sale. The goal is to build a
network of affiliates who have a financial stake in promoting your site. If you're a merchant you need to (1)
determine the commission you are willing to pay (consider it your advertising cost), (2) select a company to set
up the technical details of your program, and (3) promote your program to get the right kind of affiliates who
will link to your site. Consider two affiliate programs: (1)
Commission Junction (http://www.cj.com) sets up the
entire program for the merchant, handles administra-
tive details, and pays the affiliates. (2) My Affiliate Program (www.myaffiliateprogram.com) allows you to
track purchases through affiliate links and enables you
to administer the program yourself. More info at
www.wilsonweb.com/cat/cat.cfm?page = 1&subcat = em
_Associate.

26. *Ask visitors to bookmark your site.* It seems so simple,
but be sure you ask visitors to bookmark your site. We
use a graphic on the main entry pages to our site. See
more at www.wilsonweb.com/wmta/bookmark.htm.

27. *Devise viral marketing promotion techniques.* So-called
viral marketing uses the communication networks
(and preferably the resources) of your site visitors or
customers to spread the word about your site exponentially. Word-of-mouth, PR, and network marketing are
offline models. The classic example is the free e-mail
service, hotmail.com, that includes a tagline about
their service at the end of every message sent out, so
friends tell friends, who tell friends. More at www
.wilsonweb.com/wmt5/issue70.htm.

We certainly haven't exhausted ways to promote your site, but these will get you started. To effectively market your site you need to spend some time adapting these strategies to your own market and capacity. Right now, why don't you make an appointment to go over this checklist with someone else in your organization, and make it the basis for your new Web marketing strategy?

Index